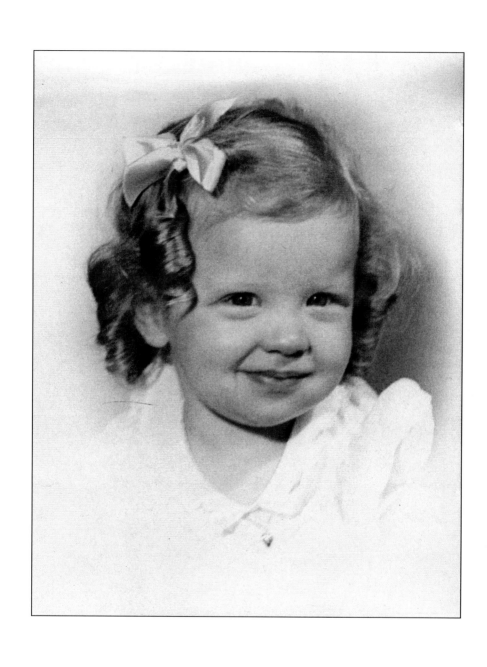

My Little Chickadee

Coming of Age in the 1940s & 1950s
Rockport, Massachusetts

by

Betty Kielinen Erkkila

Betty Kielinen Erkkila

Pre-press by North Star Press of St. Cloud, Inc.
St. Cloud, Minnesota 56302

Printed in the United States of America

DEDICATED

WITH LOVE

TO THE

KIELINEN/JACOBSON FAMILIES

and

JOHN W. ERKKILA

AUTHOR'S NOTE

In November 2000, after a fine family Thanksgiving celebration, I began pondering the subject of writing a memoir encompassing the years 1941 to 1959. Waino Ray, the author of *A Young Finn on Cape Ann*, initially inspired me by his delightful book about growing up in the Lanesville section of Gloucester, Massachusetts, as a Scandinavian-American lad in the 1920s and 1930s. So treasured is Mr. Ray's book, written now fourteen years ago, that it is rarely loaned out; it stays in a special place in my home out of visitors' view. Also about the time of the millenium, I started focusing on the term "legacy." Scarcely leaving an imprint, most people drift in and out of life's brief journey and are soon forgotten except by their families and a few friends and acquaintances.

In my Rockport school years, there wasn't a major emphasis on composition or creative writing. The subjects just weren't in vogue. I had dabbled a bit by dashing off some short articles for the high school paper, *Ebb Tide*. College years caused me to become much more interested in the power of the written word. Over time, I contributed a few pieces for the local newspaper, created a language script for a historical program re Finns on Cape Ann in the early twentieth century, originated informational sheets for a civic association, and so forth. The only "gift" that I could be leaving to coming generations would be my account of how a young girl's life was lived here in our little town. Undoubtedly, many contemporaries would have stories that fairly parallel mine.

After the Day of Giving Thanks, I started feverishly jotting down reminiscences from bygone days and decided to limit my memoir from my natal year to the summer of high school graduation. Developing text and editing only sporadically, I found that weeks, even months, would flit by with no typing nor handwriting done at all. Life seemed to intervene! During the years, I was gently and continually prodded by my husband, John. His encouragement and support are what caused me to persist in what I had to say.

The solitary and stimulating writing task seemed to never be quite done. Every time I looked at my chapters, I would alter them in some way, often adding new material. With close to a decade having gone by, the point came when I said, "No more. That's it." My part was actually finished at the end of 2009—finally. Only recently have I allowed my sisters, Shirley and Jane, and husband to peruse my work. My only caveat was that they had to be rested and in a happy frame of mind before they embarked on the nostalgic trip down Memory Lane. My siblings tell me that they are excited to have the recollections to pass on to their children. "My Little Chicadee" seemed to speak to all three of them as I had hoped; they appeared to be stirred by the contents. As for the title of the book: my cherished father often referred to me in the early years as My Little Chicadee, which I surmise was the term of endearment mirrored from the long-ago film with the same name starring screen goddess Mae West and comedian W.C. Fields.

I am optimistic that you will take pleasure in my memoir. May it encourage you to set down part(s) of your own vibrant life story as your lasting legacy!

Betty Kielinen Erkkila
Spring 2011

Prologue

Tucked away in a corner of Rockport, Massachusetts, the North Village of Pigeon Cove is a disarming place. In July and August, old-fashioned New England flowers such as statuesque hollyhocks and heavenly blue morning glories embellish picket fences and stone walls. Rainwater-filled granite quarries drizzle over the landscape. Bend-over blueberry patches gently nestle with the earth. Whispering white pines and fancy-leafed maples extend skyward. Purple loosestrife flamboyantly lights up fields, while lusciously scented magenta beach roses along the shore paths collude to entrance passersby. Halibut Point flaunts ruby sunsets and doles out spellbinding views north toward Maine and New Hampshire. The summer season truly takes one's breath away!

Luminaries and ordinary mortals alike have been enticed to this marvelous enclave fringing Sandy Bay on the sapphire-tinged Atlantic Ocean. Philosopher Ralph Waldo Emerson was riveted by Pigeon Cove's surreal seascape. Alexander Graham Bell, the telephone inventor, according to a house plaque and legend, summered here in the late nineteenth century. Sculptor Paul Manship, creator of Rockefeller Center, New York's Prometheus statue, vacationed in the village before setting up a studio nearby. The Niemi sisters, Miriam and Meri, accordion virtuosos of Finnish descent, grew up in idyllic Pigeon Cove and shared their talents with appreciative audiences from Cape Ann to Scandinavia.

Fifty or more years ago, Pigeon Cove consisted of a plethora of special buildings, including hotels, a tool company, barber shop, cobbler emporium, grocery stores, bakery, elementary school, fraternal organizations, post office, library, restaurants, churches, historic museums, and more. It was a rather self-contained, separate entity. My contemporaries and I had minimal, or no, interaction with other Rockport youngsters until Junior High School when we Pigeon Covers were integrated in September of 1953.

In order to know what it was like to come of age in a quintessential American town, circa a half-century ago, I present a memoir covering freeze frames from 1941 to 1959. If you lived during this time, may you feel sentimental and nostalgically relive it. Were you not fortunate enough to have experienced it, perhaps you will derive serendipitous pleasure from reading about these fleeting years of small town America's yesteryear.

Contents

Chapter 1
Early Years and Pigeon Cove School

Nineteen hundred forty-one (1941) was a momentous year! Franklin Delano Roosevelt was U.S. president, Joseph Stalin was named Soviet premier. The German advance on Moscow continued. Life expectancy was 62.9 years. Top movie box office stars were Clark Gable, Hedy Lamar, Bette Davis, and Spencer Tracey. Popular films included *Citizen Kane* and *The Maltese Falcon*. Postage stamps cost three cents. *The Great Gildersleeve*, a spin-off of *Fibber McGee and Molly*, debuted on the radio. Artie Shaw was considered one of the top clarinetists in the swing era. Gasoline, butter, sugar, coffee, and silk stockings were rationed. Joe DiMaggio was king in baseball. Hit songs included "Boogie Woogie Bugle Boy," "Stardust," and "You Are My Sunshine." Japanese forces attacked the Pacific fleet in Hawaii, and the president called it "a day that will live in infamy." Also that year, Betty Anne Kielinen was born.

I made my earthly entrance on Friday morning, November 28 at the Addison Gilbert Hospital in Gloucester, Massachusetts. The attending physician was Dr. Harold Baker; the nurse, Miss Josephine Polloni. Mother later told me that I was brought home to the Rockport stone house at 243 Granite Street, Pigeon Cove, on Pearl Harbor Day, December 7. Imagine how frightening it must have been for a young mother and father at that perilous time in history!

My earliest academic recollection was the Pigeon Cove School located on Story Street. A red, two-story brick building, it consisted of a teachers' room, four classrooms, nurse's office, and auditorium, housing grades kindergarten through sixth. School hours were from 9:00 to noon with a home lunch break (most mothers stayed at home) and then continued 1:15 to 3:15 p.m. On the playground were a few swings, a jungle gym, and a slippery slide. Built in 1929, the plaque outside the building read "Education Is the Chief Business of a Democracy." We amused ourselves by playing jump rope, hopscotch, marbles, and "I'm Going to Kentucky, I'm going to the fair, to meet a senorita with flowers in her hair, oh shakem, shakem, shakem, shakem if you can . . ." As late as the fifth grade, some of us thought a boy or girl could give birth to a baby!

⦿ Kindergarten was taught by Mrs. Ruth Fears. Initially, we didn't have desks but sat on conjoined auditorium seats. I began my educational journey in September of 1946 but did not actually turn five years of age until the eleventh month of that year. My school career started knowing only the Finnish language. (Finland was/is the northern European country of Sibelius, sauna, and *sisu*, the quality of perseverance.) My parents, Matthew Hjalmar Kielinen and Rachel Mary (Jacobson) Kielinen, had been born in the United States but wanted me to know the tongue of their forebears. My classmates, as I recall, included Christine MacNeil, Joel Reiter, Michael Tighe, Elana Degagne, John Swan, Homer Sweet, Cynthia Hillier, Sheila Story, Jackie Garlick, Violet Garlick, and Everett Jylkka. Sometimes as she sauntered along to class, Mrs. Fears would pluck some pretty posies alongside Mrs. Pool's white painted fence to grace her school teacher's desk.

When the school bell summoned us for grades one through six, we were instructed to line up outside the door by class, precisely, and in a straight line. Entrance would not commence until we accomplished a perfect queue.

Miss Helga Nyquist taught grade one. Bill Taylor called her "Miss Nightdrawers." In the spring, when she would be administering some sort of achievement test to a portion of the class, a few of us were allowed to go out on the playground and amuse ourselves alone, unattended. If one were a tad obstreperous in the classroom, which rarely occurred, that student would have to sit in the closet with a black cloth over his/her head. My, how things have changed! With pigtails and unruly bangs, I was excited to read about Alice, Jerry, and Jip from our Row, Peterson reader at home to anyone who would listen. When it came time for Art instruction, many a time we were handed a piece of nine-by-twelve manila paper. I often fashioned crayoned purple asters with yellow centers because Dad said he liked them. Pleasing Father was all-important.

Grade two was with Miss Eleanor Burke, prim but very kind. Each day, she trekked a mile or so from her home near the Keystone Bridge through the forest glade across Pigeon Hill. Gifted with exceptionally exquisite penmanship, she once sent me a thank you note for a present. I was thrilled to receive it. One warm day, the class was to venture on a picnic outing in the close by sun-splattered woods. Somehow I managed to forget my lunch. To the rescue, Dad drove to school with his work truck and placed the brown bag atop the classroom piano, saving the day.

Mrs. Ruth Hendy instructed grades three and four. We loved her Texan accent and the way she pronounced the words "aunt" (ant) and "salmon" (sellmen). We learned how to sing "Polly Wolly Doodle" in her class. When the superintendent occasionally visited the room, the children stood and chimed in unison, "Good morning, Mr. Cottle!" In those days, to begin the day, we had Bible readings, prayer, and a patriotic song. For literature, the class had to memorize "My Shadow," a poem by Robert Louis Stevenson. We put on a marionette show for the parents in the auditorium. My homemade marionette was Beauty from *Beauty and the Beast*. I did not know my lines very well due to nervousness and was not too confident. The teacher had to prompt me. Punch and cookies were served that afternoon. On a later day, we strolled to Balzarini's Farm on Granite Street for a field trip.

We also had to commit to heart "Flanders Field" and recite the verses to the veterans who visited at an assembly during Memorial

Day time. Memorization was quite a chunk of the learning process in those days. On the day set aside to honor departed loved ones and personnel in the armed forces, there was a band concert by adults outside of Pigeon Cove School in the morning. The American flag at that time had forty-eight stars.

When we were through with our work, we had to sit at our desks quietly with folded hands. Mrs. Hendy was a young, vibrant teacher, and we all wanted to hold her hand when she had outside recess duty.

The principal of the school was Mrs. Viola Doyle, who also taught grades five and six, a split classroom—the first three rows were fifth grade and two rows for the sixth. The class once walked to Pigeon Cove Harbor to observe a raccoon ensconced in the granite breakwater wall. We also corresponded with a penpal in Snowflake, Arizona. We had chairs and desks screwed into the floor. The desks had inkwells. The pupils (as we were called at that time) assisted by pouring ink from a large container into the inkwells. No ballpoint pens were allowed; they were *verboten*. We had to dip the sharp-pointed pen into the black ink and carefully absorb the superfluous ink from the paper with our blotters.

Every day after lunch, Mrs. Doyle would write on the blackboard in meticulous cursive writing about twenty-five sentences devoid of capital letters and punctuation marks, and we would have to use our pens, tips immersed briefly into the ink, to write the sentences correctly. Spelling bees were held often, and the competition was fun, except probably for those souls who were picked last for a team.

The school telephone was located in the hall, but I don't ever remember it ringing. Amazing! As a special treat, we could take turns ringing the buzzer bell outside Mrs. Doyle's room to announce departure time at the day's end.

I narrowly missed having Mrs. Margaret Kuhn, a stern disciplinarian (I had, instead, Mrs. Doyle for the fifth grade). Mrs. Kuhn was enraptured with the color brown and wore usually a brown two-piece suit, a brown velvet bow in her updo, and used brown ink in her fountain pen. Because the then-three-cent stamps were blue, she instead used two one-and-one-half-cent stamps because, you guessed it, they were brown. A couple years later, when Mrs. Kuhn suffered a heart attack, her charges had a substitute, and the boys "spilled" ink all around the floor. When Mrs. Kuhn returned, she made the erring boys stay in each recess and extract every bit of ink off the wooden floor. Sometimes, after a high-decibel diatribe, she banged the door into her classroom so hard it shattered the glass. As I recall, she had an after-school stamp club at her home, a former church building in the color of brown.

● There were always large decorated boxes in the classrooms for Valentine's Day. We spent hours at home during the grammar school years with Mother, creating homemade heart-shaped cards with doilies out of red and white construction paper and paste. Some youngsters had store-bought cards. I cannot forget the doleful expression on one young lad's face when he scarcely received any Valentine cards at all. Children delivered their heartfelt wishes around the neighborhood and would open a recipient's door, fling the card onto the floor, and try to flee without being observed. The house doors were usually not locked at that time; there was no need to do so. Some verses were "roses are red, violets are blue, sugar is sweet and so are you." We created, cut, and pasted for hours. What fun!

● I have retained in my mind the so-called "duck and cover" routine during the early fifties. We had to practice crouching under the desks in case of an A-bomb attack. Uncle John Kielinen, who worked at the local tool company, was told by his superiors that, if an incendiary bomb struck, it was his job to throw a bucket of sand on it! He got a big kick out of that! The Cape Ann Tool Company made a part or parts for Charles Lindberg's *Spirit of St. Louis* plane, which traversed the Atlantic, solo fashion, non-stop, in 1927.

In the elementary grades, I can remember having a plethora of drills on the "arithmetic" facts. The teacher had flashcards and we practiced with them about every day. We got to know the numerical values automatically, with no hesitation. We had basal readers such as *Friendly Village* and *Singing Wheels*. I don't recall having much of any homework, except for spelling lists, book reports, and perhaps a special report from time to time.

❧ Discipline wasn't much of an issue. Teachers were mostly idolized and had the unquestioning support of the parents. One of the "worst" offenses was talking out of turn! Not everyone, however, behaved. One name—who became a notable in town—was said to have dunked a weaker and younger male upside down with his head suspended in the toilet located in the basement of the Pigeon Cove School building.

I relished reading the Bobbsey Twins series. We could also borrow volumes from the little Story Library nearby. If my classmates and I didn't go outside on a rainy day for recess, we amused ourselves playing "Sheep and Fox." Several sheep would walk around the classroom, each with an eraser on his head. A pre-selected fox suddenly appeared, also with an eraser on his head and gave chase. We got a lot of mileage out of that simplistic game.

An anonymous individual donated a piano to the classroom. Cynthia Hillier and I took turns playing it. I recollect reading sheet music to play "Doggie in the Window" made popular by Patti Page. Mrs. Doyle also instructed us to watch Queen Elizabeth's 1953 coronation at home on our black-and-white TV, which was quite a novelty at the time.

Christmastime brought a myriad of handmade red and green chains to festively enliven the classroom. Mrs. Doyle's class had a real balsam fir tree in it. Cynthia Story, a couple of grades ahead, had to go home to take a bath because of the itchiness of the angel dust. We also lavishly decorated the classroom windows. Holiday time we had a red-and-black carol book, published circa 1935. Students were still using the book in the early 1950s with nary a problem or thought. Several of the songs were religious in nature.

We also sang from a book containing patriotic songs, religious pieces, and others such as "Maggie" and "Silver Threads among the Gold." Our music teacher was Miss Maude Thomas. One student impolitely referred to her with the sobriquet of Enormous Thomas because of her girth. There was a great emphasis on note reading and parts—do, re, mi, fa, so, la, ti, do—also the letter names of the spaces and lines of the staff with a g cleff. I was an alto. If you didn't call the names of the notes correctly, she raised her voice a few octaves. Miss Thomas unfailingly used a pitchpipe to ensure correct tonal quality.

Fifty years ago or so, many streets were blocked off for sliding during the winter. Story Street, adjacent to the school, was set aside for coasting, or sliding, as we called it, which we could do during our recess periods. Youngsters careened from the top of the hill and glided all the way almost down to the main road, Granite Street. Or we could navigate the bumpy thrills on the woods side of the school. Only one teacher supervised the entire playground!

For Social Studies, Mrs. Doyle pointed out on a map the area being studied. We'd read designated passages silently in our textbook. She had strips of paper with questions or fill-in the blanks. You got either 100 or 0; she'd record the score in her rank book. When we studied about European and Asian countries and races, the teacher informed us that Finnish (I was of Finnish lineage) people belonged to the Mongoloid race. It was surprising for me to find out, according to the teacher and the text, that I was not a member of the Caucasian race, like my other classmates. I had blond hair and blue eyes with a fair complexion and ran home and kept looking in the mirror. How could I be designated as different and not conform to what my counterparts were?

During World War II and the Korean Conflict, army trucks traveled up Granite Street to the Halibut Point area and building where there was a little "base." Because the atypical vehicles frightened me so, sometimes I sat on the curb near the Tool Company and cried. The Hirota family, which lived on the harbor side of Granite Street, was of Japanese background. They had kind of a difficult time of it. Also, Aili Hietala, married to Dad's cousin Emil and of Finnish heritage, had people unable to pronounce her surname and referred to it as "Hitler" which name was anathema, especially in that era.

As pupils we had some specialty itinerant teachers. Miss Mary (Maggie) O'Connor taught Penmanship every two weeks. As I recall, she sported pince-nez and was crabby. In the sixth grade, during one of her visits, I was turning around, chatting, while Miss O'Connor was speaking with Mrs. Doyle. Miss O'Connor then spun me around, grabbed my hand, and slammed it down hard onto the desk. Penmanship was very important, as was paper position. Everyone was forced to write with his right hand. I still picture Mrs. Fears, a calming presence, doubling as the Art teacher. For Gym we had Mr. Reed. I was not into sports/athletics.

Once when it was classmate John Swan's birthday, his father picked up party goers with his pony and cart and clip-clopped to the Swan homestead on Curtis Street. What a memorable ride and celebration! Early on, since we did not have a family car, during inclement weather days, Lucy Taylor, Billy's mother, collected some of us from school in her elegant shiny black Buick with the armrest in the back seat. It was such a treat, for our family only had Dad's work truck to ride in—all five of us, at the time.

For May Day, my school chums and I fashioned paper baskets and trundled to Haven Avenue and other damp locales to find purple and yellow dog-tooth violets, snowdrops, jack-in-the-pulpit, and pussy willows. We would leave a floral bouquet at an elder's door to celebrate spring in all her fancy finery.

The only time I recall being tardy was when Sylvia Korpi and I tarried in Phoebe Lufkin's overgrown spring garden on Breakwater Avenue to select a lavender iris for the teacher. Sylvia convinced me that the premises were deserted. Old Mrs. Lufkin knocked sharply on the window just as I was ready to snatch the flower. We raced through the woods, past the quarries, where I had been warned not to go, ever.

Mrs. Fears was presiding over the Art class that afternoon. "Where have you been?" she queried. "I don't know," I sheepishly replied. We meandered by some pits, had to slide down the slope of a sprawling boulder and gingerly walk over some mossy stepping stones teetering in the cold brook water.

En route to school after lunch, I often stopped by Melinda Mills's house at 22 Phillips Avenue. Eric Sax was sweet on her, and sometimes she rode with him on the crossbar of his bike. After school, some of us played school in Melinda's third-floor attic which had a blackboard and chalk. What an exciting time we had, taking turns, pretending to be the teacher!

One time I had severe poison ivy when I was in Mrs. Doyle's room. Because I hated to miss school, she dutifully sent homework every day. I so enjoyed all the academics. In those days, girls had to wear either a skirt and blouse or dress. Slacks were not allowed, unless under your skirt or dress. Come May, we begged Mother to let us go "barelegged" to school. When she told us we no longer had to wear winter pants, what a day of exhilaration that was!

On the way to the afternoon session at Pigeon Cove School, we passed Story's Market where I had often heard classmate Billy Taylor step in and get some items and not pay but simply say, "Charge it," as his mother did. Once I mimicked him, and Mother was horrified to get a bill later. She had no charge account there! Sometimes friends and I stopped at Niemi's store for wax lips and teeth, popsicles, fudgicles, greeting cards, and magazines with songbook lyrics. Other times some pals and I glanced at the titillating *Confidential Magazine* and an armada of other publications. Occasionally, we savored the enticing smells at Savinen's Bakery and selected an eclair, bismarck, or other delectable.

For recess snacks, we pupils consumed whole pasteurized milk from half-pint size glass bottles. Bank day was on Tuesday; I saved fifty cents each week.

Mrs. Doyle read *Member of the Wedding* by Carson McCullers each afternoon. Set in a small southern town in the 1940s, the book featured twelve-year-old tomboy Frankie dwelling in the lonely world of adolescence. The class was mesmerized by the story and was truly sad when it ended. After school on Wednesday, I attended a Pioneer Girls meeting at the Pigeon Cove Chapel. The afternoon was comprised of various craft projects, singing, Bible verses, etc.

Brownie scout meetings were held in the auditorium of the village school with Anna Persson as the leader. Each session the neatest-looking Brownie was designated as the "Slick Chick." With Mother helping with our cooking skills, we worked on diverse badges. It was there I learned to make peanut butter fudge. Sometimes at events other English-speaking mothers informally talked in Swedish which Mother didn't appreciate. She felt that they may have been chatting about her; hopefully, they weren't. In those long-ago days, there were "feelings" between people of Finnish and Swedish descent, perhaps because Finland was controlled by Sweden for about six centuries.

In winter, we dressed for warmth, not trendiness. Most family matriarchs were at-home mothers. My siblings and I donned heavy, warm pea jackets. We greeted the cold days with generous helpings of oatmeal or Cream of Wheat. I was a thickset child when huskiness was equated with healthiness.

Almost 100 percent of the families were nuclear, a mother and father with children. To mind, though, drifts in some cases of hanky-panky and deviant behavior with a minute number of parents got the village talking. Specific nomenclature was not used at that time. For the most part, in the elementary grades, we showed the stay-at-home mothers our school papers, and they gave us milk and cookies. We could and did play outside 'til suppertime, per mother's edict.

The Town Report, year ending December 31, 1947, listed "pupils" neither absent nor dismissed during the 1946-1947 school year: Pigeon Cove—Betty Ann (sic) Kielinen, Homer Marchant Sweet, Sylvia Korpi, Sandra Cream, Ann Fitzpatrick, Sylvia Mackey, Diane Spates, Virginia Hirota. Perfect attendance was a sought-after and valued attainment.

During my elementary school years, the president of the United States was Harry Truman, who vacationed in Key West, Florida, only ninety miles from Cuba. Television viewers could observe him on his morning jaunts, dapper-looking with cane or walking stick in hand, with reporters tagging along amidst the palm trees. I yearned to travel to that destination someday and happily did.

In spite of our teachers' encouragements, several of my Pigeon Cove School classmates and I were apprehensive about joining our Rockport counterparts at the Junior-Senior High School. Would we be as good, as smart? Could we measure up? I, for one, did not know one youngster from Rockport who would be in my future seventh grade class!

Chapter 2

Rockport High and Junior High School

Surrounded by maple trees, the red-brick two-story building was situated on Broadway. Junior high classes were held on the first floor; high school classes were conducted on the second. I graduated with the Rockport High School Class of 1959.

In junior high, Cora Fairbanks taught the mandatory Home Economics for girls only. She doubled as manager of the cafeteria and presided over a small staff. The ladies were busy simultaneously preparing the lunch du jour. Usually Miss Fairbanks wrote a recipe, often a dessert, on the portable blackboard in the cafeteria, read it to us, and asked if we had any questions. Then we stepped into the storeroom to collect our supplies, flour, sugar, salt in jars, and started working on our culinary skills. If we had to cook or bake something, we used the little stoves in the cafeteria working kitchen. Once we were instructed to make butterscotch candy, and I inadvertently grabbed the wrong jar of ingredients (probably not labeled by me), whatever, and mixed up the salt with the sugar. The boys taking Shop class later had a tug of war with it!

Another of the junior high teachers was Guido Piacentini. Using humor as a teaching tool for Science, he had a great rapport with the students. We learned many lessons from him. He seemed to have a lot of patience with us, but one Monday right after Easter, when the students wore their new attire the next day to school, Mr. Piacentini, irritated with Brian Carr, accidentally pulled some buttons off his new suit. I can't recall what Brian had said or done to provoke such a reaction.

Who could ever forget Catherine Churchill, my seventh grade math teacher. Her reputation for no-nonsense preceded our arrival to junior high in 1953. Nicknamed Kitty behind her back, she certainly wasn't. Every day I was so frightened to attend her class. Her insults, putdowns, scared me to death. One time, classmate Barbara Silva missed the wastebasket as we were filing out for the day and were told to empty our books filled with superfluous math papers. "Depend on you, Silva, to foul things up!" And worse.

The only time I actually saw her laugh was at me. We were studying Roman numerals. I was asked to go to the blackboard and write ninety-nine appropriately. I froze and could hardly recall my name. All eyes lighted upon me, but I did, amazingly, recall that Miss Churchill had told us that a smaller Roman numeral placed in front of a large one would have a subtractive value. I reasoned hence that it would be "IC." Since "C" equaled 100, I believed by placing "I" before it, the number would be ninety-nine. She burst out laughing. Talk about being saved by the bell. The bell rang to signal the class's end. Miss Churchill bellowed, "You're first tomorrow, Miss Kielinen!" I raced home to find out how to write ninety-nine according to her. She died on December 4, 1953, and to this day I still pause to reflect on her on that anniversary. I found out later when she had the girls only for Handwriting that she transformed into a different person, a kind human being.

John Boyle taught eighth grade English. He told us if we didn't pay better attention we'd end up as a bunch of fishermen, as if that were a terrible thing. We weren't allowed to wear lipstick in his classroom. His mother didn't wear lipstick, so we didn't need to either, said he. Being of Irish extraction, Mr. Boyle encouraged us to celebrate St. Paddy's Day. I colored my blond hair green. I did get my only A plus ever in my academic career from him. The day the report cards were passed out, I happened to be absent, which was unusual for me. One of the other students was given my report card to bring home to me. It got passed around the bus. I was mortified to get an A plus in English and laudable numerical notations in other language areas of the subject. I so desired to blend in with the rest of the crowd. When I got home, I foolishly told Dad that I only wanted to be average, not above average. Dad put me in my place saying, "When you get to be a little bit older and smarter, you'll realize that you're only average after all."

During junior high, Cynthia Hillier and I often did our homework together at her ample desk in her Castle Lane bedroom. As was the vogue in the 1950s, we had a cigarette going. If someone, her mother or father, came into the room, we quickly shut the drawer which contained the ashtray. One time, my friend and I smoked down opposite Pigeon Cove Harbor. We had so many cigarettes and so many puffs that we could hardly climb up the huge boulders to get out and home. I even smoked at my own desk at 243 Granite Street in our stone house. Again, if a family member were approaching, I'd quickly close the desk drawer. One evening, I made the mistake of blowing the smoke out the window toward my aunt and uncle's house next door. My supposed surreptitious habit ceased in short order, at least in the house, after Aunt Sylvia telephoned Mother. My aunt apparently had seen the smoke wafting toward her home.

Dances for the high schoolers were held in the Rockport High School gym. An antique lamp was placed at the chaperones' table. Generally, the boys sat on one side of the room and the girls on the other. Not too many boys asked me to dance. Once Chet Lane did, but he asked me to lead! Another time, a handsome boy came from Gloucester High School. I dreamily remember dancing with him to "I Want You, I Need You, I Love You" popularized by Elvis Presley. One dance even had some boys come down from a military base in Maine. On one occasion, Ma came in to watch us dance as freshmen and to chauffeur me home. I was mortified and felt like such a child. Reaching home, I ran up the stairs crying and told Mother that she had a daughter who was a wallflower. No one had asked me to dance that particular night!

In high school, Paul Gahm, a Dartmouth graduate, taught History. He said if you retain nothing else from his course to remember that if one is romantic he will pronounce the geographic term "Caribbean" with the accent on the second syllable. To this day, I pronounce it as a romantic would. Mr. Gahm had the college course students break up into committees to research Germany and follow up with oral presentations. I used Uncle Raymond Jacobson's scrapbook for photos of World War II. My relative had always been reluctant to discuss the Great War with all its airplane strafings; consequently, I didn't learn anything of substance from my uncle.

After school, my friend Sally Clark and I would rush to her nearby School Street home to catch *American Bandstand* on TV with Dick Clark. She had quite a crush on dark-complected, dark-haired Sal Mineo. I thought Fabian and Frankie Avalon were dreamboats and pretty hot at the time, or, in the vernacular of the day, cool.

Junior year the Spring Prom was held at the Community School from 8:00 to 11:00 p.m. The event cost about two dollars per couple. Queen that year, 1958, was Loretta Conigliari, and king was Jim Ketchopulos. My partner, John Swan, and I took part in the Grand March. John took me to Chickland Restaurant out of town afterwards in his parents' white station wagon, a Mercury.

Boyfriend Jerry Tuck and I sometimes stopped at Poole's Drug Store on Main Street for cherry and vanilla cokes or a cup of coffee. We smoked Pall Malls in the one and only corner booth. On one visit, old cigar-smoking Mr. Poole suggested that we had overstayed our welcome and it was time to move on. Reluctantly, we did. Poole's had a tin ceiling fan and a marble counter with several stools. Employee Bob Grimes multi-tasked in the popular town drug store.

A cardinal sin was being pregnant without the benefit of matrimony. During my junior year, a young student was to be in a school play. Suddenly she just seemed to disappear into thin air. Everything was hush-hush.

One rainy recess period, senior Ado Torrisi played his drums for us. We were in paradise. My classmate, Ben Hull, was able to emulate rock 'n' roller Little Richard on the piano. During some recesses, the girls did the Mexican Hat Dance in the gym or the Bunny Hop. What musical talents we Rockport High Schoolers had!

Sixteen at the time and a junior, I met Jerry at a summer dance at the Art Association. Mother had told me that under no circumstances was I to leave the dance. She would be back to pick me up at the evening's end. Jerry and I did venture across the street to Tuck's for a tonic and later down Bearskin Neck for a cup of coffee at 521 Sandwich Shop. Jazz virtuoso Sylvester Ahola often graced the dance evenings with his trumpet. Retiring in 1941, the year of my birth, he had known some dazzling entertainers such as Rudolph Valentino and Sophie Tucker and had an illustrious jazz career in London. The Gloucester Gabriel played "When the Saints Come Marching In!" during the record hop intermissions.

Jerry's parents had an upholstery truck for their interior decoration business. When he'd pick me up in it for a date, I had to sit on a crate, as there was no seat on the passenger side. On a special occasion, such as the Senior Prom, he got to drive his parents' tan station wagon, which was a treat. One snowy day (he was at neighboring Gloucester High School), we had no classes due to a northeaster, and Jerry and I trudged around Stockholm Avenue. Because the winter flakes were drifting softly down, we took refuge under a large hemlock tree with low branches on the corner of Stockholm and Oakland. Jerry kissed me under that evergreen tree, a sweet memory.

For amusement on an August day, Lynn Dean and I, an above-weight child, bicycled around Cape Ann. When we got to Plum Cove Beach in Lanesville, we paused for a refreshing drink at the water bubbler. A truck drove by with two boys standing in the open-back end. They whistled. I turned. One called to me, "Not you, dogface!" I should have known they were whistling at Lynn, who caused many a boy "to give her the eye." Sometimes I wonder who shouted those hurtful words at me.

After I got my driving license on a standard shift at sixteen, I, showing off, drove past a high school cake sale fundraiser and got too close to another car. I drove off thinking I did no damage to the other vehicle. When I got home and told Dad I grazed a vintage auto, he sternly stated, "That's hit and run." We had to go to the police station and report it. I cried, saying I would never drive again. Of course, I did.

One time I was babysitting for the children of one of Rockport's finest (police), circa 1956. The hour was late and the apartment was chilly. Somehow I discovered the recently released book *Peyton Place* by Grace Metalious atop the refrigerator. Everyone was abuzz about the novel. What a thrill! About racy life in a small New Hampshire town, it certainly was titillating for its time. It got everyone talking!

Many of us high schoolers belonged to the Tri-Hi-Y group which was organized in 1947 "to create, maintain, and extend throughout the school, home, and community high standards of Christian character." Meetings were held at the Sandy Bay Yacht Club.

Miss O'Connor, who taught business subjects and had even taught Father, allegedly asked one fellow on a warm, spring day who had removed his shirt, "What would I look like, young man, if I did that?" His answer, as the story goes: "Like two peas on a board!" "That's enough of your impudence!" she uttered. We must have all run for our dictionaries.

We never had heard of dope until freshman year in 1956. On the way to the basketball game at Gloucester High, my friends and I received news that someone had been caught with marijuana. Usage of drugs was quite a revelation and practically unheard of in my generation.

Because I was wearing braces, the orthodontist said it would be unwise to play a mouth instrument in the school band. Playing the glockenspiel, a bell-like instrument with a mallette, I was part of the R.H.S. band, which performed in the Memorial Day parade each year. Our uniform colors were gray and maroon.

Many yearbook aspirations were: "To be a credit to my family," "To be as understanding and patient as my mother," "To be cashier to a blind millionaire." Class rings were worn around girls' necks. Boys wore ties with sweaters and jackets. There seemed to be a positive correlation between dress and deportment, in general.

For Personal Typing, we had manual Royal and Underwood typewriters. The high school did finally have one electric typewriter which we typists could each use for one week during the academic year. I couldn't get any speed with it at all. Of course, we utilized carbon paper for duplicates, triplicates, etc.

The American flag in those days had forty-eight stars for the same number of states; thus forty-eight stars until the year 1959 when Alaska and Hawaii gained admittance. The last state previously added had been Arizona in 1912.

Cars for students were relatively rare in those days. One Lanesville boy drove a divine 1957 white Chevrolet BelAir convertible with a continental kit. Dave Anderson from my class had a 1954 Ford, red and white, I believe.

Rockport High School had no guidance counselors. Principal John Lane did it all. Our options were basically to get married, be a nurse, secretary, or teacher. As a female, if you had said you wanted to be a telephone repair person, you would have been spirited away. The possibilities were quite limited and very gender-specific.

Some of the fashions of the time were petticoats under full skirts, minimal make-up on one's face, jumpers with striped shirts or blouses. Several boys had crewcuts. I will expand on fashions in a later chapter.

Working on the *Rocks and Pebbles* yearbook and also the *Ebb Tide* newspaper occupied me. Memorable teachers were Madeline Rice and Roy Moore. Miss Rice often came to her French or Latin classes wreaking of tobacco. Apparently, she puffed a few drags in the teachers' room during a break. Latin aided with English grammar and vocabulary; I looked forward to her language classes. Roy Moore taught Algebra and Geometry. While I got to like Algebra, I detested Geometry. Moore also taught Psychology and Health where we encountered the word "beatnik" for the first time.

Margaret Eddie breezed into town during freshman year and conducted the Chorus. She introduced us to myriad show tunes and "broadened our cultural horizons."

Some jokes during the fifties were to telephone a drug store and question, "Do you have Prince Albert in a can? Let him out." Once I daringly called Donovan's Fish Market on Bearskin Neck. I had a crush on young Donovan and asked for a pound of fish with blond Billy Donovan wrapped up inside and then hung up. Another time, two female classmates called as many taxi cab companies as they could to pick up a non-existent passenger at a vacant house in the southern part of town. They got their kicks by watching numerous taxis converge at the property simultaneously.

The Harbormaster TV series shot in town, circa 1957, with Barry Sullivan, Janice Rule, Suzanne Pleschette, and others caused quite a frisson of excitement. Sometimes friends and I watched the shooting of the scenes around various locales and savored our brush with celebrity. Paul Burke rented a unit from my family's cottage and motel business for a brief stay.

Cynthia Hillier and I daringly got some binoculars and tried to get a glimpse of the local boys swimming sans suits, which was the custom, in nearby Mason's Pit, in the back of the Cape Ann Tool Company office property. I guess the field glasses weren't powerful enough!

Several students had a long trek to get to the school bus stop on Granite Street. A few, such as Lennie Degagne and Rose Johnson, easily walked a mile or more from the top of Pigeon Hill Street. Some girls came to school with their hair in curlers or bobby pins, wrapped with a kerchief and then combed out their tresses before class.

During our freshman year, in 1956, the oceanliner *Andrea Doria* sank off Nantucket after a collision with the ship *Stockholm*. Fellow R.H.S. student John Swan's mother was a passenger on the *Stockholm* headed for her native Sweden, but fortunately was not injured. John unilaterally decided in his mother's absence to drop his detested

Latin class with Miss Rice. Mrs. Swan was furious with his decision when she returned from Scandinavia. She hired Cynthia Hillier to tutor John in the lost Latin lessons, and he had to rejoin the class reluctantly.

During 1957, there were tremendous daily school absences from the Asian flu. Mother developed that illness. It was the only time I knew her to be sick, although she herself related that she had experienced influenza in 1918.

In our high school days, we had a gay time dancing the jitterbug, fox trot, waltz, stroll, cha-cha, and the Charleston, too. Bridget Bardot was a sex kitten and featured in *La Dolce Vita* which I never saw. *Blackboard Jungle*, a seminal movie, was celebrated and featured Bill Haley and the Comets. Haley was reknowned for his rousing song hit, "Rock Around the Clock."

The senior class girls all met about once a week for Knitting Club. I don't know of many who actually knit. We convened at various houses and smoked cigarettes, except for Sally, who apparently didn't have the need to conform like the rest of us. I can recall on one of those evenings we made merry trying to negotiate the hula hoop, a new craze of the late '50s. Having small hips, I was unsuccessful at that skill.

Curtis Waiting Station was where we got transportation home if we missed the school bus from RHS. My friend Sally Runsala and I often took the late bus so we could glimpse some prospective or fantasy beaux along Main Street.

Signe Rapp Burnham directed some dramatic productions performed at the old Town Hall as a fund raiser. I was too shy to be in any of them!

William Robinson taught English. He initiated class by saying, "Open your anthologies." We would question, "What?" I recall doing a report on author Edna Ferber and her writings.

When I graduated from RHS, I received some luggage as a gift. Wonder if it was a subtle hint from my family. Eighth grade graduation had brought a Bulova watch. Grandmother Jacobson arrived for the ceremony accompanied by Ben Gay, the linament permeating the entire auditorium.

Wearing bright-blue uniforms and hats, many of my counterparts and I were Mariners. Putting on a talent show, I recall doing the jitterbug with some others while Mrs. Ruth Anderson's nimble fingers raced over the ivories on the piano playing "Seventeen." On another occasion, Karen Johnson and I were helping leader Emma Cooper get a boat (perhaps a canoe) turned around at the Sandy Bay Yacht Club. Emma told us to warn her when she got near the dock's edge. Trying to be humorous, we didn't, and she ended up in the drink. She wasn't too pleased!

The cheerleaders and sports stars were where it was at. I was a "student." Our big rival in basketball was St. Ann's High School in Gloucester. Parent Snap Silva would bring along a bullhorn up to the third-floor gymnasium, and it caused quite a commotion. It did add pizzazz to the athletic events, though. Some well-known basketball players of the day were: Bill Hale, Honka Grimes, Everett Wayrynen, Charlie Elwell, Fred Hillier, Bob Burbank, Bob Gray, the Cleaves Brothers, etc. Cheerleaders included Sue MacLean, Louise Perkins, Cynthia Story, Mary Jane Francis, Diane Dailey, Jean Erickson, Patty Fritz, Susan Downs, Loretta Conigliari, Audrey Fears, Linda Komi, and Pat Theriault. (I wasn't into sports and would run the other way when the volleyball flew into my direction in gym.).

Rotund Edna York from Maine instructed us in English during sophomore year and was given to wearing dresses with huge flowers on them. Tom Cavanaugh often sketched pictures of her, caricatures, and passed them to me just as class was ready to begin. Given to giggles, I couldn't stop snickering at his floral renderings. Miss York would query as to why I was laughing. Of course, I couldn't tell her. Come report card time, she denoted by a numeral that I "annoyed others" in her class. Dad hit the roof! He said, "You can at least behave!" That was the only time there was any hint of improper deportment on my part!

I don't recall having much of a birds-and-bees conversation. However, I do remember reading a booklet put out by Kotex called, "Growing Up & Liking It." Some sexual information we got from our peers. Did so many older people really "do it"?

The Class of 1959 earned money for its April bus trip to Washington, D.C., and New York City over the four years of high school holding a score of fundraisers, including cake sales in front of the old L.E. Smith building on Main Street. Arriving in New York, I witnessed my first ever skyscraper. There was no alcohol on our trip to my knowledge. The Class of 1958 had about four or five students sent home hastily when spirits were discovered or found out about. The teacher chaperones didn't tolerate rule disobeyance in those days. Rules were quickly enforced! Talk about life lessons!

Senior favorites in 1959 were as follow: subject-Psychology; book-*Marjorie Morningstar*; authoress-Pearl Buck; author-Ernest Hemingway; movie-*No Time for Sergeants*; actor-John Wayne; actress-Natalie Wood; TV program-*American Bandstand*; female singer-Connie Francis; male singer-Pat Boone; song-"In the Still of the Night"; food-submarine sandwiches; fad-tights; hobby-records.

Graduation for the Class of 1959 was June 14 at 8:00 p.m. The *Town Report* stated that RHS graduated thirty-eight students. The program was as listed:

"You'll Never Walk Alone" – Senior Class – by Rogers & Hammerstein
Student Addresses – Sarah E. Clark and Benjamin F. Hull, III
Address – Dr. Hudson Armerding, Dean, Gordon College
"The Halls of Ivy" – Senior Class – "From the First Hello to the Last Goodbye"
Officers – Robert Travers, President; Vice President, Ann Broadley; Secretary, Mary Evelyn Brown; Treasurer, Michael Armstrong.

The Rockport High School Class of 1959 was equipped with many tools, academic and otherwise, to prepare the thirty-eight members for the visions and dreams of their lives to come.

Chapter 3
Homelife

Our parents wanted a better homelife for my siblings and me from what they had experienced. I lived initially at 243 Granite Street, Pigeon Cove. The land for the stone house, built in the 1930s, was given to Dad by his mother. Then the family moved to a house constructed by father and others, circa 1944, at 110 Phillips Avenue, nearby in the same village.

As youngsters, in the summer my sister Shirley and I took art lessons, using charcoal and poster paints, with Evelyn Longley, who had a gallery on Bearskin Neck called Sea Fencibles. With our camp stools and art paraphernalia, we "budding artists" strolled to various locales. Evelyn would sometimes "doctor up" our works of art.

For a time, I took piano lessons from Mrs. Fillebrown and Miss Tufts, a frail, hunched over organist (she used a metronome to aid with timing) at St. Mary's Church in town. Mrs. Speck, a later teacher, was organist at the Congregational Church. My wish was to play pop songs. She said if I could learn the classical pieces she suggested I could play any of the rock songs of the day. Teacher Speck had some fingers missing but was able to circumvent her challenge and managed ably to function as church organist for years. Lessons were held in the church vestry. I had no great sense of timing. Closing her eyes, Mrs. Speck would walk to a nearby window, expecting to hear mellifluous tones forthcoming. As I often had the irregular timing off, she was back to the grand piano in no time. Some of the simpler pieces I learned to play were: "In the Hall of the Mountain King," "Nocturne,"

"Hungarian Rhapsody," "Gypsy Rondo," and "Sonata." Sister Shirley did not like piano lessons. She wouldn't even dust the piano at home when we had to help with the housekeeping chores! As a treat, one time Mrs. Speck led me up to the steeple of the Congregational Church to partake of the breathtaking view of Sandy Bay Harbor.

As a child, I took tap dancing lessons with instructor Paul Reddy. In my memory, a recital was held at the large old Town Hall with the mansard roof. Dressed in our pale-blue taffeta costumes, we tappers danced on the stage, and I was nervous.

Flossie Hendrickson taught ballroom dance at the old Finn Hall on Forest Street when I was in Junior High. David Tupper was the pianist and Father Hendrickson the chaperone. The name of the hall in Finnish was Valon Leimu which translated into "flame of light." Flossie was a fine teacher with a pleasing persona. As teens, sometimes on Saturday nights my counterparts and I danced the night away at the hall. Chaperones sat downstairs playing cards, smoking, and drinking coffee. Actually, I don't recall seeing the adult overseers unless we ventured downstairs to the restroom. Bruce Newman remembers a Christmas tree all decorated for the holiday at one of the record hops.

Uncle John Kielinen cultivated a strawberry patch, in addition to a lush vegetable garden in a vacant plot of land on Phillips Avenue. We cousins had an annual strawberry festival with Aunt Sylvia making mouthwatering baking powder shortcakes for us and some of the neighboring children. The delectable dessert was topped with sweet dark red berries and real whipped cream. We were especially close to Aunt Sylvia and Uncle John and their daughters, Cynthia and Susan. Two brothers married two sisters; plus we were neighbors.

We didn't know our grandfathers. Grandfather Kielinen died in his forties due to cancer. Grandfather Jacobson drew his last breath because he didn't go to the doctor since it was a holiday and would cost more. Mummu (Grandmother in Finnish) Kielinen died in 1945 and Mummu Jacobson in 1961. Only Mummu Jacobson lived to be a pretty good age. The grandmothers basically spoke Finnish, although they had gone to English and citizenship classes.

During the difficult years of World War II, copious packages were sent to Finland to our relatives. Especially prized were coffee and hand-me-downs, which the Finnish relatives readily and handily reconfigured if needed.

My friends, relatives, and I ice skated on Oregon, a pond at the Witch House property with Silver Lake adjacent to it. Richard Johnson from Edgemere Road could actually jump from Oregon to Silver Lake flying through the air. Uncle John tested the ice for us. If the ice held uncle, it would hold us all. My skating left much to be desired; my ankles were weak and the cold affected me quickly. Some skaters facetiously called me Sonja Henie after the famous Norwegian skating star. They usually gave me a headstart if we had a whip in progress.

At home, our family had a beloved dog, Duchess, a boxer with floppy ears. My sisters and I sometimes pushed her in a baby carriage. Dad and Ma found the much-loved and special canine for sale at a gas station in Amesbury. We all grieved when Duchess left this earth.

Many free time hours were spent playing in the Pine House off Phillips Avenue with various designations for rooms. Our imaginations filled in the missing realities. As an aside, Dad built a lobster boat called the *Barracuda*, which he moored at Pigeon Cove Harbor.

Placing our feet into the x-ray machine, we children delighted in going to Brown's Department Store in Gloucester and observing our foot bones. We also accompanied Mother to Adasko's, Kreske's, Gorin's, and Woolworth's. Even though it was summer and hot, as youngsters, we could not wear shorts to Gloucester. It wasn't deemed proper. One had to be attired in a dress or skirt. At one time, I was a chubby girl whose clothing came from a specialty shop in Salem for portlier young people. Brown's also featured pay toilets, a nickel as I remember.

Emma Conley, *Gloucester Daily Times* correspondent, wrote about Pigeon Cove happenings in her column; e.g., who visited whom on a Sunday afternoon. She wrote of social gatherings and named the participants. Those were the good old days!

It was believed that German submarines came along the Atlantic shoreline during the Second World War. I vaguely recall blackout curtains we Rockporters had. I can picture Iiri and John Korpi visiting us on a Sunday evening. As was required, we had very faint illumination in our home. Dad was with the State Guard and had to drive around town to make sure no light was visible from windows in the area. Mrs. Garlick, Jackie's mother, supposedly spied a sub when she was up tending her child. The wooden and concrete building at Halibut Point with a cross atop the steeple was made to resemble a church to confuse the Germans, so the tale goes.

My siblings and I often wore hand-me-downs. Tudy Sawyer, Dad's bookkeeper for his plumbing and heating business, who came every two weeks and wrote out Dad's bills in pen, once gave me a gray storm coat. Colorful stocking caps with wide stripes were commonplace. Even bathing suits were passed down. Not a novel concept, recyling was fashionable way back a half-century ago and earlier. Cousin Sylvia Hietala's cousins gave me her ice skates, which were handed down to the Kielinen cousins. When poor Cousin Susan and Sister Jane got them, they were really broken in.

Doctors made house calls in those days. A patient often immediately felt better when the physician called at home. I was rarely sick, but if I were, Ma would ask, "What could I get for you to make you feel better?" I would utter, "Pineapple upside down cake." That usually did the trick! Dr. Harold Baker took a vacation at least once to the island of Maui in Hawaii. We had never even heard of that South Pacific destination. Of course, at that time Hawaii was a territory. Imagine the length of the flight in those days!

Men helped each other with building their houses; there was a reciprocity. They had what was called a "bee," and all that the workers got and expected in return was a good dinner plus the satisfaction that they had aided a neighbor in need. You could visit people, impromptu fashion, on Sunday afternoons. You didn't need an engraved invitation with a "respondez sil vous plait" for weeks ahead!

At home, Shirley, Jane, and I had to have the dreaded cod liver oil mixed in our orange juice at breakfast time to supply vitamin D. We had a handsome cobalt-blue drinking glass with an image of Shirley Temple, the adorable child actress, on it. I guess Mother thought it might make the drink more palatable.

Often policemen made their patrol rounds on foot. John Spates, the story goes, was hoping for an arrest on a particularly quiet beat. He stopped a car on the Avenues with Pennsylvania license plates. When the car's occupants were asked where they were from, they replied, "Philadelphia." Replied Spates, "Ahaaa, what are you doing with those Pennsylvania number plates?" He thought he had a live one! Apparently, Mr. Spates didn't get over the Cut Bridge, as the natives on Cape Ann would say. Jake Perkio, the police chief, ran a "tight ship." Some said he would arrest his own mother. It's admirable, though, to have high standards.

There were countless hotel fires in the 1950s all around Cape Ann. The Moorland, Oceanside, Straitsmouth, Turks Head, Linwood all went up partly or entirely in flames and smoke. The Ocean View Hotel in Pigeon Cove, however, was torn down in the 1940s. At one time Pigeon Cove was THE place for tourists to stay.

Many people fifty years ago had telephone party lines. Oh, what tidbits villagers sometimes picked up by listening surreptitiously. We had dial phones within Rockport but to call Gloucester, the operator picked up. Some residences had candlestick phones, among others. My family had a private phone as Dad had a business and needed to be accessible to his customers.

As children we did a lot of sliding (coasting) after supper down the slippery side streets, several of which were specifically set aside for that purpose. Flexible Flyer sleds were used by some, and the sliders sped down the snowy roads on cold, starlit nights.

Ma was a fabulous cook. We ate what was placed in front of us; she did not individualize the "entrees." The only concession was when Dad had liver and onions, and my sisters and I could have bacon. Meat and potatoes and some vegetables were in abundance. At times, Mother prepared cut-up fruit with mayonnaise. We never had salads nor casseroles. Everything was made from scratch. We drank milk with Bosco, probably because we noticed it was advertised on the new medium of television. Mouth-watering dessert concoctions such as frosted delights were commonplace. Mother prepared luscious fruit pies but rarely a two-crust pineapple one, which was quite special.

Once there was a Halloween party in Scouts at Degagne's on Pigeon Hill Street. Tudy Sawyer was the witch and Dottie Richardt a ghost. The ladies passed around all sorts of ghoulish objects while we had our eyes closed. Ma had to come and take me home, as I got sick from the seeming reality of it.

As a courtesy, in those days, one gave an older lady a seat on the bus. Black persons were relegated to the rear of the vehicle. We rarely saw an Afro-American, or Negro, as they were referred to at that time in history.

Some of our wonderful neighbors were the Taylor-Robertson family members who lived in a palatial, to us, mansion at 102 Phillips Avenue. The stately three-story Victorian house had multiple chimneys, a formal living room (grand double parlor), an area which would be now called a family room, two white ornate marble fireplaces, graceful staircase, enchanting veranda, ten-foot ceilings, and a widow's walk. Classmate Billy Taylor's grandparents had especially refined manners. Other marvelous and friendly neighbors were the Runsalas, Harmaalas, Korpis, Andersons, and the Hietalas. Billy Burroughs, a neighbor and reclusive bachelor, was rumored to have had stock in the telephone company. Growing up, I was friendly with Sally Runsala and also Sylvia Korpi. We had myriad pleasurable times together in those earlier years. One night Sally and I slept out on her back porch, after viewing a spellbinding World War II movie on TV.

In my teen years, I was forbidden to go into the Boogie Bear establishment, frequented by "bad girls" in Gloucester. Dad said, "Birds of a feather flock together." An untarnished name was worthy of pursuit, claimed he. He also conveyed that you are judged by the company that you keep.

I stayed over Grandmother Jacobson's Emerald Street, Lanesville home only once in the early fifties. She took care of her brood of eight children and informed Mother, "Now you can take care of your own." Two cousins and I shared a double bed in her second-floor bedroom. A chamber pot was placed under the bed in case we had an emergency during the night. In the morning, Mummu had thick Finnish *reika leipa* (bread) with heaps of butter on it. Living adjacent to Grandmother's property, Aunt Fanny and Uncle Fred still had an outdoor bathroom (outhouse) at that time.

Wrapping paper was often ironed and reused to envelop gifts. Nothing was wasted; recycling was the norm. Sometimes for an excellent supper Dad drove us to Lufkin's Diner on Main Street in Gloucester. At that time, Shirley and I sat in the middle of Dad's work truck, while Jane stood in front of Ma. No seatbelts in those days.

Noticeable sometimes in the summer months was an itinerant peddler. Toting his ample backpack and ringing his clanging bell, he would offer to sharpen knives and kitchen cutlery. The Randazza Brothers sold ice cream from their truck. I also recall an unknown man with a cart and donkey vending frozen desserts. Vega and Cushman distributed baked goods.

The Kielinen kitchen at 110 Phillips Avenue was painted blue with yellow decals. In the cellar was a freezer and a room for the assortment of preserves which Mother and Aunt Sylvia had put up. A pleasant memory is the tasty peach ice cream. I also recall piccalilli, Grandmother Kielinen's recipe, I think. Piccalilli was not high on our favorites list at that time. The kitchen had a large rocking chair. Plumbing fixtures were maroon and gray in the downstairs bathroom.

Ma washed clothes on Monday, as was the custom at that time, when most mothers held down the home fort while fathers worked outside the house. The clothing was hung on the line outside to dry. I often had to gather up the garments on frosty winter afternoons. Naturally, they were damp or wet and had to be placed on racks in the cellar to dry. Tuesday was for ironing.

The family home had an antiquated player piano. With great merriment, my sisters and I pumped the pedals furiously and played the various rolls of music. Ma left the piano sheet music all behind when we moved back to the renovated stone house. The music was out of the 1920s, 1930s, and 1940s, and earlier. One song that I especially liked was "Ramona" most likely because Dad fancied it and so I did, too.

MORE HOMELIFE

MID-TWENTIETH CENTURY, Pigeon Cove had a First National Store. Theodore Parady, the proprietor, tallied up customer purchases on the side of a brown shopping bag in pencil. Bread had a very limited shelf life in those days. Mr. Parady had a long wooden and metal claw to reach for the canned goods on the higher shelves.

Antti Niemi, whose first language was Finnish, had a shoe repair business in the Cove. I never understood how he could see to perform work in his dark emporium. One storied account had Pastor Nutting going into the shop to get his footwear mended. When Mr. Niemi asked him his name, the pastor replied, "Nutting." Mr. Niemi countered with, "Nutting? Must be something!"

Our village also boasted of the Alexander Graham Bell House on Granite Street. Apparently, inventor Bell summered there in the 1800s while working on some experiments. Cabinet maker Barbara Marshall was the proprietor of the Sawhorse Studio which advertised Pine Furniture of American Design. Ernie Philbrook was the Forest

Fire Warden and had a 1941 black fire truck which he kept on his Stockholm Avenue property. The truck is still amazingly in use by the Town of Rockport.

Ranta's, Johnson's and Walima's markets were located on Forest Street, or Finn Alley, in Rockport. Years ago, many food stores delivered orders. On the same street was a Lutheran Church which had church services in Finnish only for decades. Aunt Sylvia and Uncle John hiked there from Pigeon Cove on some nippy Christmas mornings for a worship service. They then stopped at Mari tati's (Aunt Mary's) for after-church *nisu* (Finnish coffeebread with cardamom) and coffee.

Circa New Year's Eve 1958, unfolding into 1959, there was a celebratory party at Jerry Tuck's house on High Street. Since his good-natured parents were ensconced upstairs, as teen revelers we had the run of the lower level. The living room was dimly lit, and we did a lot of cheek-to-cheek dancing, listening to records and stealing a kiss or two. The 45 rpm record was spinning "Smoke Gets in Your Eyes" while we were all dreamily slow dancing in the darkened space. All of a sudden, the fire alarm came blasting in. The oceanside Straitsmouth Inn was ablaze! We party-goers rushed to the conflagration. Dad, a volunteer fireman, requested dry socks. All the firefighters and their wives were later feted with a supper evening by the owners, even though not much was left of the inn except for the dining room/kitchen portion. According to a previous guest, a lady named Dorothy Wilson, who had vacationed often at the hotel, one's seat location in the dining room depended on how long a tourist had been staying at the inn. It took several years to get a window seat with an ocean view!

Wonderfully nostalgic steam trains left Rockport Station for Boston. On a rare occasion, our family chugged to the capital for a circus, a Cisco Kid rodeo or to view Cinerama. The smell of the cinders flying through the air was uniquely unforgettable.

There was no diversity in Rockport. We were shocked one summer's day to spy a black man jaunting along the town's main street.

Our maiden Aunt Laila knit us lovely sweaters and mittens. Even, once, a jumper for me. When I was in the first grade, I was embarrassed to have something homemade and yearned for a store-bought outfit. So no one would notice my jumper, I kept my sweater buttoned all day long, even though the classroom was stifling hot.

Aunt Laila was employed as a domestic and cook at the Phillips Estate in East Gloucester. Mr. Phillips had a high position at LePage's Glue. When my sisters and I visited the mansion, we applied Aunt Laila's lipstick and pranced around in her high heels playing pretend. The kitchen stove had various colored lights on it. Their telephone number, as I recall, was Gloucester 25. We called our aunt on a Sunday afternoon after she had finished the mid-day dinner dishes to take an auto ride with our family. We Kielinens and Aunt Laila meandered through the country roads in the two-door, second-hand gray Dodge Coronet, which had been owned by a Ranta fellow who had died of a heart attack.

In the summer, my siblings, Cousins Cynthia and Susan Kielinen, and I had swimming lessons at Front Beach. Evelyn Suutari was instrumental in helping us to learn to paddle and backstroke. Of course, we couldn't go swimming for an hour after eating. If we were going with Mother and Aunt Sylvia, we waited not so patiently under the giant oak tree, and then Ma drove us in our one-time green station wagon to Cape Hedge or Pebble Beach. Before starting back home, we all stopped at a tiny ice cream concession nearby for a welcome cooling sugar cone. Also, I learned quite a bit about swimming at Camp Cherith, a Protestant church camp in Alfred, Maine.

Shirley, Jane, and I had definite curfews, and no sassing was ever permitted either. Sometimes I had to sit in the corner until Dad came home for lunch or supper. Mother warned, "Maybe he can talk some sense into you!" Dad never hit us, but Ma sometimes pulled our hair. Dad seemed to control us by telling us how disappointed he was in our behavior, which was usually sassing back. It worked! Dearly wanting to please our parents, we were very malleable.

In 1957, a real-life Gloucester teacher was hit over the head in her Granite Street, Pigeon Cove home. She had told someone in the Gloucester diner that she had just been paid or someone overheard her telling someone else. I was so scared and wanted Dad to start locking the doors of our house. Because he couldn't find the house keys, we had to place the rocking chair at a certain angle to secure the back door. We started locking our car door after that, too, because Dad had heard someone try to start our Dodge at 2:30 in the morning.

The neighborhood children of the era made their own amusement and were seldom bored. Spring and summer brought Giant Steps, Red Light, softball, hopscotch, jumprope, marbles, and croquet. Shirley, Jane, and I even had a tent on a platform, said tent later taken over by airwigs! All the rage was painting by numbers on trays and wastepaper baskets. What works of art, so we thought!

The Granite Street Balzarinis (not to be confused with the Curtis Street Balzarinis) had a winter sleigh and horse for milk delivery. Looking back now, it made for quite a picturesque scene on a snowy February day. Town men stood in the back of trucks with shovels and threw sand over the slick roads. Cars had chains on the tires, too.

In the Bolton area, my Cousins Joanne and John (Nonny) and I swam at Fort Pond. In the mid-fifties, polio was quite a scare as I remember. The Tervo property had cows grazing in the back of it. One bovine had a bell around its neck, waking me up each morning with its jangling. I recollect the summer night dance party Aunt Anna and Uncle John had in their backyard with variegated lights strewn about the premises.

The Raivaaja, a Finnish newspaper published in Fitchburg, came into countless Finnish-American homes, bringing news from the homeland and telling of activities in the Fitchburg area and including Cape Ann. My parents were born here, but an aunt and some of the uncles were delivered in Finland and later came to the United States as young people.

Mr. Bloomberg, the Jewish haberdasher, drove around Cape Ann selling his wares out of a black panel truck. He wisely learned the rudiments of Finnish, selling to a passel of door-to-door customers; it was a smart thing to do.

As mentioned earlier, doors were not locked much in the 1940s and 1950s. One family in Lanesville regularly left their back door open for the milkman, Mr. Young, to place the bottles directly into the refrigerator. A handwritten note suggested that he also help himself to a piece of freshly baked apple pie at the kitchen table.

Mummu Kielinen, Laila tati, and baby Johnny Kielinen, just under six months, upon death, all rested at uncle's family home at 239 Granite Street. Black flowers were customarily wreathed on the front door indicating that the family was in mourning.

Dad had a garden which Oscar Johnson from Pigeon Hill Street tilled for him. Our father planted rhubarb, which my siblings and I didn't particularly like, and strawberries, potatoes, stringbeans, spinach, and more. Ma and Aunt Sylvia made sweet jelly from the purple Concord grapes clinging to the wooden arbor.

Dad called me "My Little Chickadee," an endearing form of address. Perhaps it was after the W.C. Fields and Mae West movie of the same name; I'll bet it was!

Homes had underground garbage pails. Once a baby raccoon was caught in one in our yard and couldn't get out. The poor helpless creature was enveloped with smelly, spoiled garbage. Finally, someone suggested I get a boat oar and carefully open the cover. Miraculously, the little raccoon was able to climb out and knew where to find its mother beyond the huge moss-covered boulder.

Dad was one of the youngest master plumbers in the state. He changed his vocation when he was about thirty-eight years of age and went into building and creating dwellings for sale or renting.

Our parents attended dances at Pythian Hall, Finn Hall, and took part in supper club dinners. They often went for Saturday night outings with Marion and Karl Johnson and had many happy evenings.

Irene from Stockholm Avenue took care of us. We eagerly awaited for her boyfriend to arrive by bus from Gloucester to visit her. We watched them "making out" on the living room sofa. John Korpi also babysat for us. We threw pillows down the stairs at him. When our behavior with him got around to Mother, our comportment improved rapidly.

Johni seta fished off Andrews Point. My cousins, siblings, and I breakfasted on the rocks with Sylvia tati cooking bacon and eggs over a fire in a large pan. We gazed at starfish and sea life in the tidal pools. At times, we roamed through the woodland paths with Uncle John, who made whooping sounds and pretended that there were some Indians in the area. We clung to our uncle's side for dear life!

Sometimes four or five cousins would go riding with Doris and Frank Harmaala, a childless older couple, in their 1949 black Buick sedan. On one outing, they instructed us to order whatever we desired at the Dock Square refreshment stand. Taking them at their word, I, a chunky child, whose clothing came from a Salem specialty shop, ate two hamburgers, chips, ice cream, tonic, you name it! Then we would drive to watch the progress of the A. Piatt Andrew Bridge on Route 128 in Gloucester. Andrew was the founder of the American Field Service, an area congressman, and also a one-time Economics professor of Franklin Roosevelt's at Harvard University in Boston. For a splendid Christmas excursion, my parents took us to ride on Cape Cod's Edaville Railroad. Brilliant holiday lights sparkled as our train car wound through cranberry bogs.

A legion of men from Pigeon Cove proudly and honorably served in various military branches during the Great War. These patriotic individuals were and are listed on the honor roll in the village square. Some whom I personally remember include: Niilo Makkonen, Arthur Olson, Toivo Wiberg, William Ranta, Jacob Ranta, Carlton Story, Isabel Reed, Jorma Savinen, Walter Wayrynen, Edward Bailey, Wain Baker, Robert Bernard, John Huttunen, Melvin Olson, Henry Shewbridge, Benton Story, Theodore Watters, John Balzarini, Miriam

Conley (later Seppala), Arline Erickson (later Ranta), Pingree Hillier, Edward Jylkka, Nestor Lahtinen, and Reino Makkonen.

With the prism of a half-century, the homelife our nurturing and loving parents gifted my sisters and me with seems idyllic. We lived in a secure environment with neighbors exhibiting friendliness, caring, and civility. My counterparts and I could actually have a real childhood before transcending into adulthood. How lucky and blessed we were!

Chapter 4

Church

The Pigeon Cove Chapel on Granite Street was an integral part of my life. There I attended the Sunday School, Teen-Agers Youth Fellowship (TYF), Pioneer Girls, Colonist and Explorer groups. In addition to the regular church service, when I got older I also took part in the Sunday evening observance.

In Sunday School, we became familiar with the Ten Commandments, the Twenty-Third Psalm, and other verses. I was presented with a Bible on June 1, 1952, as were others, for learning pre-selected Biblical verses. Noted on the presentation page was 2 Timothy 2-15 "Study to show thyself approved unto God, a workman that needeth not to be ashamed, rightly dividing the word of truth."

If we recited our pieces well at the annual Sunday School Christmas program, Dad said he would take us to glimpse the glittering outdoor light display at the O'Connell Estate on Eastern Point Boulevard in Gloucester. We practiced our parts with Mother over and over again. Everyone from the Cape Ann area gravitated to the palatial mansion to view the elaborate, scintillating show!

In summer, my sisters, cousins, friends, and I attended Daily Vacation Bible School where we were required to memorize Biblical verses and sing songs and hymns of praise and rousing choruses. On one outing, the staff took all of the attendees for a picnic to Half Moon Beach in Gloucester. Some youngsters got to ride in the open back of a large truck. The pastor's wife, Lois Draper, was very involved in Chapel activities during the mid-fifties. Having a lovely soprano voice, she was very musical and witty, too. Ruth Johnson, a parishioner, volunteered to go to the parsonage and do up the dishes and make the beds to help out Mrs. Draper during Vacation Bible School days.

For five years, starting at age sixteen, I was the organist at the Pigeon Cove Chapel which was Protestant. Mrs. Draper instructed me in the rudiments of the pipe organ instrument. To the congregation's chagrin, the Drapers were leaving their ministry at the Chapel around 1958. Her husband, Bob, was a charismatic leader of the membership while wife, Lois, played the organ and often offered angelic-sounding solos.

At a later time, Mrs. Isabel Tharp volunteered to sing some solos with my organ accompaniment. She claimed that she had sung at Calvin Coolidge's inauguration. Unfortunately for me, she always seemed to select the most difficult pieces, sometimes with four or five sharps. At times, due to a hearing challenge, Mrs. Tharp would be in the wrong key and ask me to start over again during the morning church service. Finally, she was told gently by the pastor and the music committee that she would have to conclude her singing. It seems that some parishioners were refusing to attend services.

One Christmas, our choir performed excerpts from the *Messiah* by Handel. June Spaulding and her mother ably presided over the Senior Choir. Mary Jane (Critchett) Lane capably led the Junior Choir. She had such a sweet manner about her.

As young people, we were forbidden to go into a Catholic Church in those days. When our youth group members were roller skating or ice skating out of town, near Boston, we once came upon a Catholic group at the rink; we had to leave and go elsewhere. There would be no commingling. That happening left quite an impression on me! Dancing was frowned upon. It was important not to wear suggestive or provocative attire in any way.

Pastor Draper took us teens on several happy activities, once at least to a Gordon College pond for ice skating. Only three of the TYFers went to Crane Beach in Ipswich for sun and frolic. Another time, the Teenage Youth Fellowship group traveled to Canobie Lake, an amusement park in New Hampshire. Lynn got into the Rumpus Room car at the Fun House, which was dark and convoluted inside, with a male stranger. The minister, rightly so, was furious, the only time I ever saw him angry.

Nick Woodbury, a Gordon College student, the brother of the youth director's wife, played the trumpet and sometimes the piano too at church services and Sunday School. I had a crush on him with his blond mane and quick fingers racing over the black and white ivories of the piano. The youth leaders at various times were Doug Elliott, Ray Bergen, and Peter Polloni. Mostly they were Gordon College seminary students.

Easter sunrise service was held at Pigeon Hill on top of Landmark Lane. The ocean almost surrounded us, with Old Sol slowly dawdling out of the colorful horizon. We triumphantly sang songs of the resurrection such as "He Lives" and "Christ Arose." The view from the hill was truly panoramic. A waffle breakfast followed in the church basement with Mother and Sylvia tati sometimes helping out. It was the only time we got to have the breakfast favorite all year long. I think our home waffle iron was broken.

One Easter, choir member Charlotte, who expressed that she resembled the much-married actress Elizabeth Taylor with her chestnut tresses and violet eyes, was supposed to sing a solo part with the Senior Choir. She chose, instead, to make a grand entrance in her flowered picture hat and jaunty ensemble down to the front of the church, just as the service was to begin. The choir director, June, was incredulous and livid; she had to sing Charlotte's part!

As young teens, Cousin Cynthia and I were invited on a car trip to Rumney, New Hampshire, to the summer home of mother and daughter choir members, the Spauldings. En route, we were served Spam sandwiches, which were horrid to my taste buds. I was gagging trying to down the little snack. June and Bernice asked us how we liked the sandwiches. Cynthia and I were sitting in the back seat of the car and, not given to prevaricating, I warbled, "I've never had anything like it!" We were ready to burst into uncontrollable laughter. I put the remainder of the sandwich into my pocketbook, and there it stayed all weekend. I couldn't even place it into their wastebasket at their northern vacation home. They surely would have spied it as they emptied all the trash prior to our departure. The Spauldings, well-intentioned as they were, could be termed "helicopter hosts," hovering over us constantly!

The youth group often ventured out Christmas caroling. Sometimes I brought along my glockenspiel and struck the bell-sounding metallic bars with a mallette. We were invited one year to Ruth Fears' seaside home to behold her resplendent holiday tree. Real, lighted candles shimmered on it as they did years ago. She said her deceased husband, who had been with the fire department, would have rolled over in his grave and had a fit if he knew she was lighting genuine candles on the tree. Mrs. Fears had a handy bucket with water and extinguished the ribbons of light in quick order.

My sister Shirley and I took part in a religious retreat for young people at Camp Cherith in Alfred, Maine, for a week. There I learned to swim in the nearby lake. The counselors were assigned bird names. There was much Bible reading, prayer, etc. We had to wash the dishes by hand after our meals and would later have a "midnight snack." Sister Shirley had to be picked up by our parents before the week's end; she was homesick. When Ma and Dad arrived, they brought along a black-and-white glossy photo of Julius LaRosa which had come in the mail to add to my movie star collection.

The Pigeon Cove Chapel provided my sisters and me with many worthwhile and enduring spiritual experiences and lessons.

Chapter 5
Holidays

The major holidays were celebrated with numerous family members joining the Kielinen family. Uncle John and Aunt Sylvia and their daughters, Cynthia and Susan, were sure to be part of the convivial events.

On Easter, prior to church, we found that the hip-hopping bunny had stopped by earlier, leaving pastel baskets overflowing with candy. We five cousins usually had outfits of navy, pink, or lavender. Photos were taken to remember for family scrapbooks a half-century later and beyond. Mid-morning we attended our church service. The altar was filled with a profusion of white lilies and other happy and fragrant harbingers of spring. Hymns of triumph were sung out in rejoicing fashion. The junior and senior choirs prepared special music for the important day.

The chapel sponsored a sunrise service atop Pigeon Hill overlooking New Hampshire and Maine. One time, Cousin Cynthia was laughing while singing as part of a vocal trio. Her mother was mortified and told her and the other two choristers to face out to the ocean because Cynthia's father's boss, Mrs. Edith Dean, the owner of the tool company, was in attendance.

After Easter dinner, which generally was a succulent ham or turkey, would follow decadent desserts and a walk, often beyond Pine Pit toward Lanesville, by the children and menfolk, while the mothers stayed behind to wash and dry the dishes. Garbed in their showy finery, many Cape Ann families paraded along Stacy Boulevard in Gloucester in the afternoon. Young ladies wore seam nylons and pristine white gloves and hats with veils to complement their outfits. Contests were held for the spiffiest garments and prizes were awarded to families with enviable style. Inexplicably, I never attended the walk on the boulevard.

On the Fourth of July, we Kielinens generally had a typical New England meal consisting of salmon, new potatoes, peas, and blueberry pie for the finale. Friends Toini and Eino Koski often were visiting from Staten Island, New York. When we were younger, my siblings and I had to take a pre-parade nap, although it was difficult to sleep. Dad often helped to carry the firemen's net to collect money from the parade watchers. Beforehand, we parked on Forest Street and trundled over to Dad's aunt's for coffee and a short visit.

The night before the Fourth, an outdoor dance for adults was held at Central Fire Station. The engines were moved out and bright multi-colored lights were strung around the building façade area. There was dancing from 8:00 or 9:00 p.m. to 1:00 a.m. inside and outside the station. On July 3rd, there was a fund-raising bake sale in front of the General Store on Main Street. Years ago, there were demonstrations of model planes and track meets, too.

In decades past, the 7:00 p.m. Independence Day parade started at the railroad station—six divisions, military, fraternal, merchants, pet, horribles, and fire kits with two bands. Fire Chief Guy Thibeault was the grand marshall. The local band regularly paused and played a stirring march at Dr. Earle F. Green's front porch on Broadway as an affectionate tribute to the esteemed physician. Post parade, professional vaudeville acts enthralled at Back Beach's Legion Hall gazebo. A food tent was available on the grounds. Later a "monster bonfire" with an outhouse perched atop would be torched off. Remnants of real outhouses were still commonplace fifty or more years ago.

Christmas was a much-awaited and celebrated holiday. Many families in those days mailed out greeting cards with their names pre-printed, which was quite a novelty. December 24th, Christmas Eve, our kith and kin gathered for a festive smorgasbord containing Finnish meatballs, eggnog, *lipia kala* (smoked fish), rice pudding, golden brown *nisu* men, and gingerbread women with raisin eyes made by Sylvia tati. Joulu Pukki (Santa Claus) visited good little girls and boys. Great excitement and anticipation rang out!

Grandmother Jacobson celebrated with us, along with aunts, cousins, uncles. Uncle John Kielinen, or alternately Dad, mysteriously had to leave on Christmas Eve to pick up a jar of cream. We never made the connection; they were Santa! One Christmas I received a bicycle as a gift. My parents asked me to demonstrate my riding skill as the streets were devoid of snow. I didn't know how to apply the brakes and went flying down Ocean Avenue and wound up in the thicket on lower Phillips Avenue. Another holiday time, my sisters, Shirley and Jane, and I received a dollhouse, a petite toy piano, and magic slates, which were a big hit. A favorite present was a bunny fur set, also a gold pen that wrote in three colors, red, blue, and green. Once a neighbor, Ilmi, gave me a pair of underpanties as a Christmas offering. I was an overweight child but was insulted by the size, which was way too big for me. My sisters, cousins, and I delighted in delivering gifts to the Humlins, Ed and Esther Jacobson, Jean Jacobson, and Wayne Jacobson in Johni Seta's vintage auto.

The 78 rpm record player blared out the numbers "I Just Go Nuts at Christmas" or "I Saw Mommy Kissing Santa Claus" or "Rudolph the Red-Nosed Reindeer" by Gene Autry. December 25, as dinner accompaniments, we had vegetables galore and every imaginable pie. No consideration was given to calories or cholesterol. Like the Pilgrims at a three-day feast, the diners returned on the day after Christmas for encore presentations and sometimes the day after that, too.

For the Christmas of 1958, Sally Runsala and I decorated her Uncle Charlie Balzarini's wintergreen tree in his Granite Street living room. He now lived alone in the family homestead, and we thought that he could use some holiday cheer. Before the demise of his parents, Charlie's relatives gathered almost daily under the leafy trees on a long bench for afternoon coffee and conversation. People had time for each other in those days.

Tuck's Drug Store featured parti-colored homemade ribbon candy for sale. Santa came in his sleigh on December 25th morn, if there was snow (otherwise in a horse-drawn wagon), down Cove Hill to Dock Square to hand out cloth bags containing fruit, nuts, and candies/cookies to the eager young people. A bus transported some kids to the town center from the Pigeon Cove School.

At Pythian Hall, we looked at the same holiday movies every year, but it didn't matter to us. Antonio "Niggy" Balzarini was jolly Santa, and he exited the upstairs hall via the outside fire escape. I plinked the piano for carol singing. We lads and lassies were also treated to ice cream hoodsies. When you licked the cover, there was a famous person's image visible. Uncle John also brought the Kielinen cousins to the second floor of the old Town Hall for a Masonic holiday party.

In the late 1950s, neighbor Billy Taylor did a creditable impersonation of Elvis Presley for us all on Christmas Eve. Uncle Walter was awestruck. Once Bill gave my sisters and me a bottle of treasured Chanel No. 5 perfume to share. Another holiday, my cousin gave Dad two jars of ink. It didn't matter that he didn't own a fountain pen. We also reluctantly had our younger sister Jane's red and green chains encircling our redolent evergreen tree.

Our Christmas contrasted greatly with Dad's Pigeon Cove family holiday in the 1920s. According to the oral history of Uncle John, Dad's brother, family members tramped into the woods to cut down a tree, hopefully a white pine. It was placed into the "sitting room," which was not heated in the winter. There were real white candles on the tree which were only illuminated when their mother was present. For gifts, one would get fruit, often wrapped in red tissue paper and a pair of socks knit by Mother. Old socks that had missing elements were repaired and the children got them back as Christmas presents. The red tissue was also created into homemade ornaments for the special tree. The description by Uncle John makes their Christmas celebration sound starkly and simplistically beautiful. Family and togetherness was all.

Above: A Kodak moment in front of the Pigeon Cove School on Story Street mid-twentieth century—probably Memorial Day morning when a band traditionally played. Left to right, back row: Betty, Sylvia Korpi, Cousin Cynthia, friend Lana, Sister Shirley; front row: Cousin Susan, Sister Jane.

Jane, Shirley, and Betty pose for the photographer at Willie Winkle Studios in Ipswich, circa 1949-1950.

Betty (with pigtails) and Shirley (embracing a stuffed animal) with their parents in a 1940s family portrait taken inside our 110 Phillips Avenue home that Dad and others built. Notice the Finnish rug on the floor.

Dad's grammar school in Pigeon Cove (corner of Cathedral Avenue and Phillips Avenue), probably in the 1920s. Dad is in the middle row, third from the left. Young girls' hair bows and high-button shoes were in fashion.

The stone house in winter dress that Dad and others created from granite quarried from the premises at 243 Granite Street, Pigeon Cove.

Above: Sister Jane and our beloved boxer dog, Duchess, circa 1950s.

At left: Swashbuckling Uncle Theodore "Cleo" Jacobson, nattily dressed, admiring friend Onni Erkkila's Harley Davidson motorcycle in 1939.

Birthday celebration at 110 Phillips Avenue. Left to right, front row: Cynthia Wayrynen, Janice Johnson, Jane and Susan Kielinen; middle row: Lana Tuomivirta, Shirley Kielinen, Sally Runsala, Cynthia Kielinen; back row: Karen Johnson, Esther Jacobson, Betty Kielinen, Elana Pistenmaa, Sylvia Korpi.

Shirley, Jane, and Betty in their pinafores on a summer's day in 1950 aboard the *Mount Washington* boat on Lake Winnipesaukee in New Hampshire. Rarely leaving Cape Ann, the sisters still recall that wondrous day.

The Couples Club, mostly relatives, met yearly from the 1930s through the 1940s to celebrate collective anniversaries. Ma and Dad are to the right in the first and second rows.

Loving cousins on a summer's day in the late 1940s. Left to right, back row: Ed Jacobson, Esther Jacobson, Joanne Tervo, Betty Kielinen; front row: Cynthia Kielinen, John Tervo, and Shirley Kielinen.

Taken on April 1, 1951, this snaphot shows Sister Shirley, friend Lana Tuomi-virta, Cousin Cynthia Kielinen, and Betty, perhaps getting ready for Sunday School at the Pigeon Cove Chapel. Note the in-teresting chapeaux.

Our family's two-door gray Dodge Coronet, purchased from an estate, 1950.

Grandmothers Mary (Ranta) Jacobson and Sanna (Koivisto) Kielinen watch over the apple of their eye, baby Betty Anne in 1941.

First cousins Betty, Cynthia, Esther, Joanne, and Shirley happily show off their two-wheelers. Jane and Susan sit Indian-syle in front.

The Kielinen family spent a memorable afternoon visiting Dad's aunt and uncle, the Nestor Kielinens, in Gardner, Massachusetts. Left to right, back row: John Kielinen and wife Sylvia, Aunt Laila Kielinen, Rachel and Matt Kielinen; front row: Cousins Betty, Cynthia, Shirley, Susan, and Jane.

Built about 1860, the Lane School in Lanesville, in the early years housed eight classes. Mother's family once lived in a little house in the diagonal rear of the school. Date unknown for the photo, which was given to the author by Mother's early childhood friend, Adeline Ahonen.

At left: Mother and Father joyously pose in front of their first home after their April 25, 1936, marriage. Their reception was at the popular Finnish Wainola Hall.

Below: World-class musicians in photo, possibly taken in 1940s. Left to right: Miriam Niemi, an admiring friend, Sylvester Ahola, and Meri Niemi. The Niemi Sisters were accordionists extraordinaire while "The Gloucester Gabriel" was a world-class trumpet virtuoso. Sylvester from Lanesville often entertained during dances at the Rockport Art Association record hops in the 1950s.

Circa 1920s, the Jacobson family's formal portrait. Left to right, standing: Walter, Fred, Toivo, Grandfather; seated: Sylvia, Cleo, Anna, Rachel, Raymond, and Grandmother. Notice the large bow on Rachel's head and the younger boys' sailor attire.

Betty with her adored sisters, Shirley and Jane, in 2008 at a summer party.

Five Kielinen cousins balanced on a seesaw in 1950. Left to right: Jane, Betty, Cynthia, Shirley, and Susan. Uncle's yard also had five swings for the quintet.

Quarry Workers' International Union of North America Report for March 5, 1920, Lanesville, Massachusetts. Read the plethora of Finnish surnames. Grandfather Jacob Jacobson is member #3233.

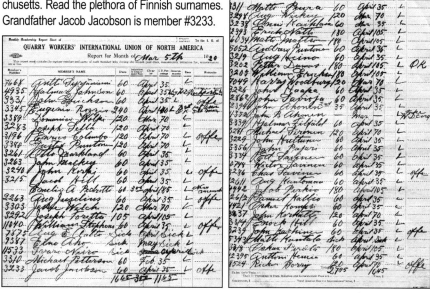

Circa 1946, Ruth Fears's kindergarten class at the Pigeon Cove School. Author spoke only Finnish upon entrance. Left to right, back row: Violet Garlick, Jackie Garlick, Sheila Story, Cynthia Hillier, Homer Sweet, Everett Jylkka; front row: John Swan, Lennie Degagne, Michael Tighe, Joel Reiter, Christine MacNeil, and Betty Kielinen.

Cousins Andrew and John Jacobson, eldest of the first cousins, of Springfield, Massachusetts.

The Matt Kielinen family standing in front of the 110 Phillips Avenue house.

A pensive proof of Betty, who graduated from Rockport High School with honors in 1959.

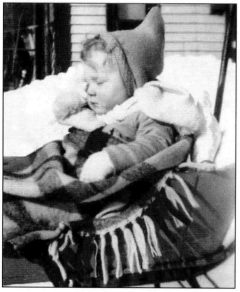

Cousin Wayne Jacobson sleepily dreamily awaiting winter sleigh ride, circa 1948.

Lanesville Lutheran Church Confirmation Class—late 1920s. Father Matt Kielinen sits in the front row, second from the left; Aunt Sylvia is in the back row, second from the left. Dour-looking Pastor Ronka conducted lessons for the confirmands all in Finnish.

Chapter 6

Jobs

An early job as a young girl in the 1950s was waitressing at Sunset Inn, a three-story affair owned by Henry and Margaret Shewbridge in Pigeon Cove. Henry fried the bacon for a component of the bountiful breakfast. Margaret orchestrated the kitchen doings, with a cigarette dangling out of her mouth, while preparing appetizing food for the summer visitors. A white uniform worn by the waitress was de rigueur. I helped by setting the tables with dishes and utensils. Each guest, who was assigned a specific seat in the dining room, had an individual napkin ring encircling a cloth serviette. The waitress had to remember who sat where. Everyone had the same breakfast items or dinner entrée. It was my task to ring the little hand-bell in the living room where the "summer boarders" were eagerly congregating and announce "breakfast is being served" or "dinner is being served" in the evening. A charming custom.

Joan Capillo had been the waitress at Sunset Inn but was leaving for nurses' training, and I took her place. One time another waitress, Mary Ann Toppan, ready for a cool quarry or ocean dip after work, appeared with her white uniform clearly displaying the silhouette of her bathing suit underneath. Mrs. Shrewbridge was not amused! After waitress duty, I helped Henry with chambermaid work. Some guests stayed two weeks or longer and left excellent tips at the end of their vacation.

Oleana Restaurant in Rockport, where I waitressed for a few summers, had Phil Amero as the head chef; he was very patient. The eating establishment was known for its smorgasbords featuring Scandinavian foods served by brightly costumed waitresses. In the fifties, the staff didn't have nor use calculators. We actually had to compute the front and back of the guest check, and the sums had better agree and come out correctly. Quiet, bald Bill, who helped in the kitchen, had a flirtation with one of the waitresses. The waitress's husband showed up one evening unannounced. The situation was a bit touchy for a while. Stern Jackie Hubbard flipped tasty hamburgers with pan fried onions on the grill. Patience was not one of her virtues. Chuck Francis, an efficient college student with a brown crewcut, was in charge of cashing up and closing when owners Ida and Chrip Corliss had the night off. Once when I was working behind the counter I accidentally spilled a frappe on Chuck's brand-new suede shoes. Amazingly, he wasn't upset at all.

Linda Cunha, Anna Beloff, and high schooler Cynthia Sheldon were also employed by Oleana's. I recall Cynthia going around the corner, just out of view of the public, to study from her French book. Oleana's hired an affable adult employee from Gloucester who was instructed by the owners to place lettuce on all the sandwiches, unless otherwise specified. One surprised customer was served a peanut butter sandwich laced with lettuce!

Competent Marcia Mallette with short chestnut curly hair waited tables. Other employees included Sheila Day, Russell Allen, Don Nikola, John Maki, Mady Currier, Ben Hull, and Christine MacNeil, and several others, including sister Shirley. The majority of the restaurant staff consisted of young girls and boys attending college and working for school tuition.

Oleana's had a marvelous ninety-nine-cent luncheon special featuring three Swedish meatballs, mashed potatoes with gravy, a small green or jellied salad, rolls, raspberry or coffee jello with whipped cream, and coffee. What a deal! The Corlisses would never give out the proprietary Swedish meatball recipe. Mary Alice Francis, Chuck's mother, was my first and frequent customer. I've never forgotten her calm demeanor. During my first nerve-wracking days at the position, serene and collected Mary Alice was made to order.

One summer's day, Candy MacDonald got a lift for her work hours with a young fellow in a convertible. Naturally, upon arrival at Oleana's, her blond curly locks were windblown and in disarray. Mrs. Corliss scolded her, saying, "Young lady, you march yourself right down back (to the then restroom) and comb your hair and put on some lipstick before you start your shift!" Oleana's had standards worth emulating.

Con and Zelda Green were year-round employees and gave 100 percent to the restaurant. The waitstaff plucked mint for the iced tea from the beachside of the building. Vi Makkonen Luster, Anita Walima Littlefield, and Don Upham, a humorous jack-of-all-trades, also worked there for lengthy periods.

The area restaurants did not serve coffee prior to your meal arrival in those days. Coffee was brought to the table with a breakfast entrée. All the food, day or night, was superb. Oleana Restaurant was so busy that it had to close its doors for a half-hour before lunch was served to restock napkins and other supplies. A long line of customers often could be seen waiting with happy anticipation several buildings down the street.

The Corlisses had a Pontiac Star Chief black convertible which they housed at Broadway Garage. Sometimes they let employee Don Upham drive it. Some of us were filled with envy!

Tahti Mand, a minister's daughter studying at Smith College, waited tables at Oleana's. The family was originally from one of the Baltic Republics, Estonia. Her native tongue was similar to Finnish. In the Finnish language, her name meant "star." Tahti and some college mates, Pat and Mary Lou, would start their tan base coat at Back Beach, which was less populated than people-packed Front Beach. When their tans were sufficient, they debuted at Front Beach. The Smith College girls once rented a camp in town and seemed to have a certain aura of sophistication in the eyes of us townies.

One unforgettable snippet concerned Jerry, a boy who had a crush on me and vice versa. He worked at his parents' Tuckraft business in the Granite Shore Building across the street from the restaurant. At the counter he ordered a fruit turnover and a cup of java. Together the items would have totaled twenty-five cents in 1958. I got so ruffled that as I passed the turnover on the plate to him, it slid into the open mustard jar. Jerry gave me an eight dollar tip! I must have been some waitress!

Another time, a female summer boarder, who wore a generous flouncy picture hat, plunked herself down on the counter stool. I never saw her eyes but did notice that she had ruby red lipstick on and a cigarette hanging out of her mouth. Prior to eating, she took out her false teeth and wrapped them in a napkin. She left and headed into the restroom. I had to run after her, knock on the bathroom door, and blurt out, "I think you forgot something!" Was I embarrassed! She didn't seem to be!

A male customer, perhaps a sexagenarian or septuagenarian, who was nearly blind, often came into the dining room. He wanted me to hold his hand while he gave his breakfast order (I was sixteen at the time and quite innocent). He romanticized, "If I were younger, etc." He was so visually challenged that he shuffled into the restaurant kitchen once when he was exiting. At the summer's end, he requested my name and address, and I gave it! In late autumn, a black wrapped package arrived for me with no return address. Was it an explosive device? Inside was a stunning oil painting in a gold frame by the artist, a autumn scene which I cherish to this day.

One adult breakfast waitress could never seem to add up the customer's bill correctly. She often asked me or someone else to help. I had to compute her guest checks and mine, too. We had to do the math in our heads in those days. No calculators had we!

Waitresses wore spotless white uniforms with pastel-colored aprons, often aqua. If one had a long head of hair, health standards dictated that you wear a hair net. The Lady with the Feather, a local newspaper reporter, came to the counter one noontime. Chatting with a countermate, she dallied for such a lengthy time, not touching her plate of food any further. I removed the plate and placed it around the corner with the other unclean dishes in the bar tray. Later she had me retrieve it, and actually finished her lunch!

Other restaurants in Rockport in 1958 were: Peg Leg, Headlands, and the Blacksmith Shop. Some of the prices at Oleana's were and are ingrained from that mid-century decade. Norwegian Rosette, a pastry shell with custard sauce and strawberries, was twenty-five cents; a donut, eight cents; coffee, ten cents; milk shake, twenty-five cents; apple pie, twenty-five cents; pecan pie, thirty cents. Named for the Corlisses' dear daughter, Lobster Christina cost $4.95 and was the highest price on the menu.

I was hired on Valentine's Day 1958 and was a bit anxious at the interview. The owner, Ida Corliss, had a classically lovely apartment over the restaurant. She did put me at ease though. One noontime, one of the teen waitstaff, on a little piece of food-ordering paper designated for the chef, wrote "1 delicious sweet scallops" as was listed on the menu. The chef declared, in an effort to get her to abbreviate, "I know they're delicious, I know they're sweet—"1 scal" would be fine to write." We all had much to learn. I also put in time at the counter after school during the winter months. Oleana's was a very busy establishment.

Artist Iver Rose, who often painted clowns, always left a liberal tip. Christine Fields, country-smart looking in her pinafore jumper and wide straw hat, was dropped off in Rockport by her husband in the beginning of the summer and picked up at the end.

One time, Dot Soini, the elegant hostess with gray hair fashioned into a twist, and I sang "Happy Birthday" to a party and got a big-hearted tip.

At the end of the season, Oleana employees had a party generally at busboy John Maki's house on Bianchini's Pit in Lanesville. A couple years after graduating from high school, I had my 1955 green-

and-cream four-door Chevy 210 with a standard shift and drove to the season's end celebration. John in later years purchased the restaurant.

My sisters and I were chambermaids at our family business, Boulder Top, cottages and motel overlooking Sandy Bay. Jane and I were planning to get t-shirts with "Boulder Top" imprinted on them, but sister Shirley claimed it probably would be misconstrued, reminiscent of the Victorian rooming house at the junction of Five Corners called House of Clapp owned by the Clapp Family.

At our Boulder Top motel and cottage business, once a guest flushed lobster shells down the toilet and caused, you guessed it, plumbing problems, with the toilet overflowing and water leaking into the ceiling of the unit below. Another time, two University of Massachusetts professors were entertaining their boss with a barbecue at their rental unit. Our boxer dog filched the broiling steak from the hot grill and raced off with it. I don't remember what the indignant renters did to substitute! I think Mother had to rush to the grocery store for a replacement.

Quite often I did some babysitting. In those days, a sitter received fifty cents per hour. When I sat for the Hamiltons, they would turn down the high-in-the-wall thermostat before they left. They had a pregnant relative visiting from one of the Dakotas. There was no mention of a husband. Motherhood sans husband was very "shhh" in that era.

Also, an early job of mine was shelving books at the town's Carnegie Library. Irene Wilson and Margaret Pearson were always very helpful to me with my numerous filing questions.

My world of work was both educational and eclectic. Not only did I assimilate a multitude of skills, but I met some fabulous people, some of whom are still my friends to this very day.

Chapter 7
Fashions

A s is the case today, celebrities of the 1940s and 1950s were utilized in magazine ads to promote products. For example, with Cashmere Bouquet soap, the inference appeared to be that if you, too, used said soap perhaps you could look like or resemble the pictured movie star. Fads come and go, and the forties and fifties were no different.

ID (identification) bracelets with photos inside were all the rage in the 1950s, as were autograph books. My autograph book, received from Cousin Wayne Jacobson, in 1953, was put into good use during the early years of the decade. Babysitter Irene included: "How YY's UR, How YY's UB, UR 2 YY's 4 me." A friend scrawled: "All girls love their brothers But Betty so good has grown That she loves other girls' brothers Far better than any she could ever own." Another inscription was: "When you get married and live by the lake, save me a piece of your wedding cake." A saying in some autograph books that I heard about was: "True friends are like old china, precious, rich and rare; false ones are like autumn leaves, found everywhere."

America has long had a love affair with the automobile. The well-admired 1956 Ford Victorias had plenty of scintillating chrome on them. Shiny silver metal was pervasive. In those by-gone years, some cars that were on the road included Packard, Hudson, Kaiser-Frazier, Willys, Edsel, Studebaker, and Nash. The fifties were the era of the dramatic pointed fins. New cars typically had covers placed on seats to keep them soil-free. A few of the vehicles in the 1940s had running boards. Driving lessons were offered at Rockport High School on a standard shift. When I got my first car, a 1955 Chevolet, as a late teen, Dad apprised me that we were working people and working people drove Chevys or Fords, not Buicks!

Fripperies of fashion of the time included girls wearing gold crosses and pearls around their necks, pageboy hairdos or ponytails, and minimal make-up. Bobby socks with sneakers or white bucks, saddle shoes or penny loafers were de rigueur. Hair bands, plaid fabrics, faux flower corsages, DA's (duck's ass haircuts for boys), fur balls, boleros, and fake collars (dickies) with v-necked sweaters could be spotted. Bobby pins covered by a kerchief were all prevailing for the younger and older set. Kerchiefs were commonplace and tied under the chin. It was perfectly acceptable to go out into public with one's hair in curlers or bobby pins enwrapped with a kerchief.

Millinery shops seemed to abound. A well-attired woman's outfit was topped off by an interesting and striking head piece; hats were worn by both genders. Ladies' chapeaux were often focal points, with flowers, fruit, and feathers, really artistic confections. Veils often covered a fraction of the face. *Glamour Magazine*'s editorial message to readers one year in a mid-decade of the twentieth century was: "More often or not, a fresh and flattering hat is the best spring tonic any girl could take; it will bring new sparkle to her eyes." One spring Mother bought a new hat, one that she thought was smart-looking and eagerly modeled the chapeau for Dad, who burst out laughing. She exclaimed, "You paid for it!"

Van Raalte nylons were in vogue. The seam had to be carefully placed in the center of one's gams; it could be quite a task. Aunt Sylvia had sixty-gauge nylons—whatever that meant. I never figured it out. Ladies wore two-piece nylons with seams and suspants and sometimes girdles, especially if one was more robust-looking. Girls and women wore gloves, sometimes with a pearl button at the wrist for punctuation. The glitterati of the golden era showcased décolletage and the requisite white gloves. A well-dressed woman wore high heels, the higher the better.

As cigarette smoking was very much accepted, often women and teen girls lit up. At one time, hard as it is to believe, even medical doctors advertised for cigarette brands which were thought to be healthful. The furies of smoking were not known; it was a mark of pseudo sophistication, we thought. Lucky Strike's motto "It's Toasted LSMFT Lucky Strike Means Fine Tobacco" appeared at the bottom of the package. Some of my Rockport junior high classmates facetiously claimed that LSMFT stood for "Loose Sweaters Mean Floppy Tits." The advertising for Lucky Strike featured legs only visible beneath the cigarette package with a prancing, dancing girl.

Olive-skinned actor Sal Mineo sported a cigarette rolled up in a t-shirt sleeve or behind the ear. Of course, fellows across the land emulated the star's habits. Marlboro cigarettes were well-known. Boyfriend Jerry and I smoked Pall Malls. Somehow, my girlfriends and I were becoming aware of our budding sexuality and managed to put an erotic twist onto just about everything.

An issue of *Glamour Magazine* in 1953 admonished readers on hair salon manners, "Do not smoke while your operator is dressing your hair. Your reaching for an ashtray makes it hard for her to work. And smoke in her face can be very annoying."

Haircoloring was considered not acceptable; it was trashy or cheap according to many. Does she or doesn't she questioned the hair coloring product Clairol ads. The hair salons often had a plastic curtain surrounding the customer; of course, everyone was aware of what was going on. One Pigeon Cover, brunette Bertha Toppan, had colored her hair very light blonde and didn't want her mother to know. When she left the house for school in the early morning, she had her hair in curlers and kerchief and it appeared the same when Bertha returned at day's end. In between, for class, her fair locks were on blatant display.

Light & Bright by Richard Hudnut home hair lightening was used by many teeny boppers. A single application could be applied directly to your hair to lighten and brighten a little or a lot depending on how many times one used it. Ma claimed that I ruined the veneer on our bathtub by its application. I was a natural dishwater blond but craved blonder hues. Blondex also removed dingy, dirt-laden film from one's hair.

I had naturally curly hair and regularly got a feather razor cut from Miss Elaine's or Mrs. Margaret Anderson's hair salon on Main Street. At times, I lamented about my unruly curly mop. Ma said my hair was my best feature and I should concentrate on some real deficiency. Braids were in style, too, especially perched high on one's head. Girls wore petticoats under their wide skirts or dresses. Some females used hoops, although I never did. If one's slip was showing, a friend hopefully announced it by whispering, "It's snowing down south." Brassieres came under the unmentionables category.

The boys had crewcuts or a DA in the summertime, a baldie, a whiffle or a daring tomahawk. A tomahawk would surely cause endless comments. Grown men topped their heads with caps, hats or fedoras.

Paper dolls and doll houses were in fashion, as were submarine sandwiches and pizza in the culinary department. Those foods were novel in the 1950s. One's wallet held multiple photos of beaux, family, and friends. With the slightest encouragement, out would come the pictures for a showing.

Teen-age girls and young women often wore Tangee natural lipstick. The name was short for tangerine. Orange in the tube, but when applied onto the mouth it complemented one's lip tones. Customers could purchase it at the five-and-ten-cent store; Tangee debuted at cosmetic counters in the 1930s! Helena Rubenstein was also a sought-after brand of lipstick and nail polish.

Circa 1958 when the chemise dress look was chic, I headed to a Saturday night record hop at Spiran Hall in a pink and white-striped dress with a large pink bow and generous white collar. Dad said my outfit looked like a nightgown! I thought I looked dapper, cool, and spiffy. I was taken aback by his assessment.

Words and their etymologies are always fascinating. Some words for our vocabulary included swanky, gay (happy), catty, hawk (as in steal), and beauty parlor. Charm bracelets were also everywhere in the 1950s.

Elvis Presley, the icon who scandalized adults with sexy, smoldering looks and sounds, was said by some to be a "new low in spiritual degeneracy." He appeared on the *Ed Sullivan TV Show*, televised from the waist up. Millions of fans will surely recall his early hits "Hound Dog" and "Don't Be Cruel." Adults/parents thought his undulating hips were too seductive.

Candy bars that we devoured were Mars, Snickers, Three Musketeers, Old Nick, Clark, and Baby Ruth. I had seen Snickers advertised on TV and asked Mr. Parady, the proprietor of the First National in Pigeon Cove, to stock the delicious candy, and he complied.

Going steady was all the rage. High school rings were worn around a schoolgirl's neck on a chain. Many young ladies did not kiss nor allow themselves to be kissed for a few dates to gain respect from the fellow. During swim season, no bikinis were worn but rather a modest two-piece or one-piece bathing suit. More seemed to be more at that time in the fifties.

Teen girls sometimes wore sedate two-piece dress suits, punctuated with a faux flower corsage. One year I had a navy blue suit and Shirley a medium blue. Later we switched and thought we looked rather snazzy. Completing the suits were black patent leather shoes worn before Memorial Day and white shoes during the summer months.

Photos of movie and TV stars decorated the wall of my bedroom. Phyllis Peterson handed down her 1940s collection, which included Sonny Tufts, Errol Flynn, Van Johnson, the affable boy next door. Later I foolishly ended up giving the picture collage to neighbor Lana, who later gave the assortment away. It would have been really special to own it now!

Noxzema or Cuticura soap was advertised as being beneficial for curing acne. Modess and Kotex were for menstruation. As mentioned earlier, a booklet entitled "Growing Up and Liking It" came to our home in a plain wrapper for my perusal by Mother. It was somewhat embarrassing to chat about coming of age with one's mother!

Sheath dresses were seen everywhere. Rolled-up dungarees, shorts, pedal pushers, topper coats, cufflinks, and headbands were all seen in the 1950s. Culottes or skorts or skirts were also worn for summer comfort.

Prevailing fashion at the time encompassed pointed bras and cinch belts, sweaters with the buttons laced down the back. A woman's magazine of the era advertised a strapless bra "to uphold your charms in comfort." If your charms were insufficient, you could always stuff tissue paper into the cups to increase the measurement. Some "bad girls" wore falsies, which were padded with foam rubber. Once I did use some tissue to accentuate my assets. A girdle advertisement proclaimed, "The most amiable elastics coddle your curves, cloud-soft fabrics tuck you in tenderly."

Sartorial styles included Ship-n-Shore blouses in color combinations of pink and gray. Blackwatch plaid frocks were time and again included in stylish wardrobes. Madras and Bermuda shorts were in demand, too. In the late 1940s, voluminous skirts were greatly in evidence. Christian Dior was an idolized name in fashion.

At-home mothers garbed themselves with aprons just about every day. Aprons helped one's housedress to stay pristine. Generally the apron covered the entire front of a figure, with a piece encircling the nape of the neck. If company or guests were coming, often only a half-apron would be worn, frequently a fancier "model."

Looking at antiquated, sometimes faded, photos is always a nostalgic pastime. It seems one can rather accurately denote the decade by observing the hair styles and the fashions of the day. Each era had its distinctive charms!

Chapter 8
Movies, TV, Songs

In the heyday of the fifties decade, the price for an adolescent's Saturday movie matinee in Gloucester was fifteen cents at the Strand Theater and twenty cents for the North Shore. Ushers at the theaters used flashlights to seat patrons. Sometimes they had to discipline the moviegoers, too. Once my beau and I sat purposely in the back row so he could puff a few drags on a cigarette when the usher was out of view. Often my girlfriends and I would attend a Saturday afternoon movie. One of the first cinematic memories was *The Quiet Man* with Maureen O'Hara and the legendary John Wayne. In those days, theater attendees got a good value for their money, newsreels of current events, cartoons, preview of coming attractions and much more.

Some of the Hollywood movie studios at the time were MGM, Paramount, Warner Brothers, RKO, and Twentieth Century Fox. Idols of the silver screen in the 1940s and 1950s included Gary Cooper, Humphrey Bogart, Burt Lancaster, smoldering Montgomery Clift, James Dean, the teen favorite who perished in a fiery Porsche auto crash at age twenty-four. Dean made quite a lasting cultural impact. Fans were besotted by Marlon Brando, Van Johnson, Kirk Douglas, and Gregory Peck. Other dreamboats, in the vernacular of the day, were Rock Hudson, Robert Wagner, Russ Tamblyn, and Tab Hunter, also a vocalist in a version of the melody "Red Sails in the Sunset."

Louella Parsons, Hedda Hopper, and Sheila Graham wrote gossip columns about the celebrities. The movie magazines, including

Modern Screen, Silver Screen, and *Photoplay,* kept the public enlightened by the goings on of the stars. Later we found out how scripted everything was for public consumption! Marriages were sometimes even arranged!

Glamor girls and glitterati in the forties and fifties were ubiquitous. There was a frisson of excitement about screen goddesses such as Betty Gable, the leggy pinup girl of World War II, Lana Turner, Rita Hayworth, Ava Gardner, Jane Russell, high wattage Marilyn Monroe, and femme fatale Sophia Loren. Some classic-looking actresses in all their cinematic glory were Greer Garson, Doris Day, the girl next door, and Ginger Rogers, who tripped the light fantastic with Fred Astaire. The fifties also presented Ann Blyth, Jane Powell, Debra Paget, Kim Novak, the short platinum-cropped actress who often dressed in lavender shades, Hope Lange, Diane Varsi, Tuesday Weld, and Sandra Dee, the teen queen and America's sweetheart who starred with dreamboat Troy Donahue in 1959's *A Summer Place.* She later wed singer Bobby Darin. The couple made quite a celebrity splish splash, but the marriage sank. Other stellar personalities included dancer Cyd Charisse, Betty Hutton, Robert Mitchum, Charlton Heston, and Dean Martin and Jerry Lewis, zany comedians extraordinaire.

Mae West in the 1950s of "Come up and see me sometime" fame was still popular as were Alan Ladd and Veronica Lake with her peek-a-boo hairstyle. Ingrid Bergman of Sweden hit it big here in the United States and caused quite the scandal, while still married, with her illicit romp with a lover on the island of Stromboli, located off the coast of Sicily.

Tinseltown stars wore real fur coats, especially mink, which seemed to be synonymous with polish, style, and sophistication. They had trendy designer outfits, jewelry, coiffures, and often posed with cigarettes. The famous dress designer was Edith Head, who herself, ironically, was usually clad in the most austere of manner, generally in forgettable black. Unforgettable Carmen Miranda with her inimitable froufrou hats looking like colorful fruit baskets and smiling eyes entertained audiences everywhere. As with the legends of today, the stars depended upon the artistry of hairdressers and makeup wizards to transform them into alluring creatures.

Hollywood royalty Grace Kelly, a cool blonde originally from Philadelphia, left the U.S. to marry her real-life prince, Rainier of Monaco, in the mid-1950s. She and her entourage traveled to the principality via the ship *USS Constitution*.

Holiday time in 1954 Uncle John took my cousins and me to view *White Christmas*, a charmingly simple and innocent story, starring Bing Crosby, Danny Kaye, Vera Ellen, and Rosemary Clooney. The fabulous choreography of the chanteuses in their bright red and white fur-trimmed costumes was magical.

About 1952, Lucille Ball originated her screwball comedic TV program which swept across the land. She and husband, Desi Arnaz, had to sleep and be televised in twin beds on the set even though married to each other in real life. They couldn't use the word "pregnant." A strict moral code was in full force at that time.

Drive-in movie theaters were all the rage in the 1950s. Some car drivers would sneak their pals into their auto trunks so as to save on the pay-per-person entrance charge. On a sultry, summer's night, my aunt, uncle, and cousins in Bolton and I saw *East of Eden* with maverick bad boy, James Dean. We cousins were so excited to be able to stay up 'til 1:00 a.m.

Screen gems which I recall viewing and the approximate years were:

1954 *Magnificent Obsession*
1955 *Marty, Rebel Without a Cause, Giant, Picnic*
1956 *Friendly Persuasion*
1957 *Peyton Place*
1958 *Auntie Mame, Teacher's Pet, South Pacific*
1959 *Some Like It Hot* with Jack Lemmon, Tony Curtis, Marilyn Monroe; *Pillow Talk* with Doris Day (who wore sumptuous designer outfits) and Rock Hudson; and the epic *Ben Hur*.

Bathing beauty Esther Williams was choreographed in several aquatic movies swimming and diving gracefully.

Addicted to and relishing all the Westerns on TV, I was often kicked out of the house by Mother on a Saturday morning after household chores. Some of my favorite cowboy stars were Hopalong Cassidy, the Lone Ranger with a black mask and his sidekick, Tonto, Roy Rogers and Dale Evans, Cisco Kid, Gene Autry, Guy Madison as Wild Bill Hickok, Jock Mahoney as the Range Rider, and Bill Williams as Kit Carson.

Other TV favorite shows were *Super Circus* with baton twirler Mary Hartline, canine capers with *Rin Tin Tin* and *Lassie*, the *Pinky Lee Show*, and of course *American Bandstand*. Sally Clark and I rushed to her School Street address after class to catch the various couples dancing in Philadelphia and then tried to imitate the latest dance crazes such as the stroll, which I never mastered!

Some in-demand and well-received songs of the mid-twentieth century were: "A You're Adorable," "Mule Train" with Frankie Laine, "Buttons and Bows" with Dinah Shore, "Near You," "You Always Hurt the One You Love," "Paper Doll" with the Mills Brothers. "Chattanooga Choo Choo" by the Glen Miller Band was and is a forties musical classic.

Of course, the epitome of the singing icons in the 1950s was heartthrob Elvis Presley. He was the talk of the high school and had teeny boppers swooning in every secondary school across America, I'm sure. He really had us all shook up! His smoldering sensuality and hypnotic voice and eyes had us swooning over "Love Me Tender" and other songs which still thrillingly resonate today.

Other in-demand tunes of the early fifties included "Tennessee Waltz" and "Mockin' Bird Hill" by Patti Page; "Stranger in Paradise" and "Love Is a Many Splendored Thing" by the Four Aces; "Sh-Boom" and "Earth Angel" by the Crew Cuts; "Ain't That a Shame" by Pat Boone and Fats Domino; "Tutti-Fruitti" by Little Richard; "Only You" by the Platters; piano rendition of "Autumn Leaves" by Roger

Williams would make me feel melancholy in a lovely and lonely way; it was hauntingly beautiful.

The mid-fifties brought "Honky Tonk, Part I," by Bill Doggett; "Standing on the Corner" with the Four Lads; "Green Door" with Jim Lowe; "Singing the Blues" with Guy Mitchell; "My Prayer" by the Platters; "Whispering Bells" by the Dell Vikings; "Little Darlin'" by the Diamonds; "My Special Angel" by Bobby Helm; "Party Doll" by Buddy Knox; "At the Hop" by Danny & the Juniors; "Old Cape Cod" by Patti Page; and "Honeycomb" by Jimmie Rogers.

Teens of the time jitterbugged and fox-trotted at record hops with spinning of the 45 rpm platters at the Finn Temperance Hall or at Spiran Hall or the Art Association in the summer amidst some classic-looking statues and works of art, which we were not particularly interested in at that time.

Commercial establishments often had juke boxes. You inserted your money and depressed the names of the rock 'n' roll songs of the day that you wished to hear. A Gloucester diner, the Hesperus, had table juke boxes, which one could play while schmoozing with friends and savoring some good food at a reasonable price.

The late fifties produced "La Dee Dah" by Billy & Lillie; "Rockin' Robin" by Bobby Day; "Little Star" by the Elegants; "Do You Wanna Dance?" by Bobby Freeman; "Susie Darlin'" by Robin Luke; "Purple People Eater" by Sheb Wooley; "Stagger Lee" by Lloyd Price. Also, "Venus" by Frankie Avalon; "Love Potion # Nine" by the Clovers; "Seven Little Girls" ("Sitting in the Back Seat") by Paul Evans; "Mr. Blue" by the Fleetwoods; "Teen Beat" by Sandy Nelson; "Personality" by Lloyd Price.

Boyfriend Jerry's aunt did try to round out our musical tastes. She squired us to Methuen to listen to renowned organist, Virgil Fox. Music teacher, Margaret Eddie, at Rockport High also acquainted us with sundry show tunes.

Television was a novelty in those early days of the 1950s. We couldn't get enough of the new-to-us communications machine that would rock the entire world. Many of us sat night after night in the neighboring Korpi family's little living room to view mesmerizing programs. The Korpis were among the first in the area in town to own a TV. Parents Iiri and John graciously hosted us and never suggested it was time to leave or they heard mother calling!

Some of the wholesome and winsome programs I recall taking delight in watching were: *Colgate Comedy Hour*; Paul Winchell with his puppet (Winchell once vacationed at our family's Boulder Top); the fabled Milton Berle; *You Bet Your Life* with Groucho Marx of the famed brothers of madcap films. We also tuned into Herb Shriner, Amos & Andy, black entertainers, and Red Skelton.

Other TV shows that my family watched included: *I Married Joan; Ozzie & Harriet* with their fledgling, handsome pop singer son, Rick Nelson; *My Friend Irma; Jackie Gleason Show*, which was telecast live. Once Jackie on a *Honeymooners* episode fractured his leg on the show, but the scene had to continue (there were no retakes). Also *Stu Erwin Show*; singer Jane Froman; *Dragnet* with Jack Webb; *Meet Millie; Our Miss Brooks* with Eve Arden. We also reveled in *Life of Riley* with William Bendix; *Make Room for Daddy; George Goebel Show; Father Knows Best; Loretta Young Show* with her glamorous couture creations; *Mr. Peepers* starring bespeckled Wally Cox; *Private Secretary* with Ann Sothern and *My Little Margie* with her hilarious, nutty antics. All the shows offered good, clean productions fit for the whole family. Those were the days!

Of course, we adored *Howdy Doody* with Claribel the clown, Mr. Phineas T. Bluster, Princess Summer, Fall, Winter, Spring et als as youngsters. The mid-fifties presented *December Bride* with Spring Byington; *I've Got a Secret; Gunsmoke; Midwestern Hayride*; also the *Steve Allen Show; Tennessee Ernie Ford; Alfred Hitchcock* with his spellbinding, glue-you-to-your-seat mysteries. I rarely saw *Perry Mason*; usually I was off at a record hop on Saturday nights.

I Remember Mama was a much-loved sitcom my family couldn't miss on a Friday night. Based on Kathryn Forbes' book *Mama's Bank*

Account, it recounted life with the Hansens, a closely knit Scandinavian family living on San Francisco's Steiner Street in the early twentieth century. Wholesome, good entertainment.

My sisters, at least one of them, and I stayed up to watch *Your Hit Parade* on a Saturday night if we could when we were early teens. Usually we had babysitters on that date night for our parents. Early regulars included Dorothy Collins, Snooky Lanson, Russell Arms, and Gisele MacKenzie, who crooned the latest songs of the day.

Arthur Godfrey's TV Show included entertainers Carmel Quinn, Janette Davis, Julius LaRosa, Marion Marlowe, Frank Parker, Lu Ann Simms, Haleloke, the McGuire Sisters, the Chordettes, the Mariners (one of the few racially integrated vocal groups that regularly appeared on TV), Pat Boone, a then college student at Columbia; Anita Bryant. Julius LaRosa was fired publicly, on air. In one of the most widely publicized incidents in TV history, Godfrey told a stunned audience that LaRosa was singing his swan song. Thereafter, as I recollect, Godfrey's ratings greatly diminished.

Reminiscing about all the songs, movies, and TV shows of the 1940s and 1950s takes me wistfully down Memory Lane. They were magnificent decades!

Chapter 9
Kielinen/Jacobson Families

My immediate family consisted of five members, Dad, Ma, sisters Shirley and Jane, and me.

One of eight children of Jacob and Mary Jacobson, my mother, Rachel Mary (Jacobson) Kielinen, was born in March 1913 in a tiny house behind the Lane School in the Lanesville section of adjacent Gloucester. The family surname was originally Prepula in Finland but changed to Jacobson in Lanesville. In those days, a person often took the name of the owner of the home in which he was residing. Also, because the Finnish names were difficult to pronounce, often the quarry bosses assigned new and easier ones. Being one of five boys and three girls, Mother certainly didn't get a lot of attention and had to help out for the common good of the family. She related that many families of the 1920s and 1930s had twelve or more children! According to Mother, her family was small by what was considered to be the norm.

Her fifth grade class, instead of being at Lane School, in the heart of the village, was held at the Finnish Wainola Hall, the site of numerous plays, concerts, athletic competitions, and weddings. (Due to a runaway grass fire, the hall burned inadvertently, circa 1947.) Ma told the story of being left in the classroom, which included a pot belly stove, with classmate Adeline Ahonen. The pair was locked into the room by the teacher, Miss Collins, who left for her lunch break. The other children tramped home for a hot meal or sandwiches. Depending on who told the story, either Adeline or Mother knocked over the teacher's ink jar while chasing the other around the room. Ink spilled all over the teacher's desk and her papers. That was the last time the duo was allowed to stay in the classroom for lunch!

Ma also reminisced about the music teacher giving her a ride on the instructor's sled from Mother's Emerald Street home area to the multi-purpose hall on Langsford Street. As a youngster, mother and her counterparts often had to resort to wearing Pillsbury flour sacks, stylishly sewn into rather attractive apparel, we years later discovered. They roller skated at The Rink in the village and sometimes watched silent movies accompanied by appropriate piano music befitting the action on the screen.

Ma worked for the Ely Family as a nanny to son, Peter. (Father Edward Ely was married later to the character actress Jean Dixon, who was especially known for appearing in the 1936 classic romantic film entitled My Man Godfrey, starring William Powell and Carole Lombard.) According to Internet information, Ms. Dixon debuted on the Parisian stage with Sarah Bernhardt while still a student at a French university. (A nonagenarian lady in the Cape Ann area relates that movie star Joan Crawford sometimes came to the Annisquam section of Gloucester to visit with Jean Dixon.) One time Mother had to race into the beach water at Ipswich Bay, uniform and all, to rescue and pull in little rambunctious Peter, her charge. Aiti (Mother in Finnish) only traveled to Gloucester, from the Lanesville "suburb," for the very first time when she was twelve years old and thought she was in a big city! The village of Lanesville had all that most people required.

Ma also was employed by the Dewey Family of Newton and Annisquam. On one occasion, Ma asked the Newton house doyenne for a small raise for her domestic services. Mrs. Dewey said that she couldn't afford it. Ma countered with, "Darn funny you can afford to have all those tea parties!" Momentarily stunned, Mrs. Dewey replied, "Well, well, I get invited back too!" Ma, being surely a fine employee, got her raise. Aiti had a certain pluck that would serve her well throughout the remainder of her life!

Ma talked for years of getting lost in Boston's Chinatown while working as a maid at 232 Franklin Street, Newton. Her female friend was planning on staying to catch another movie at the theater. Because she was so far off from the employer's mansion where she resided in one of the servants' upstairs rooms, Mother had to be put on a streetcar by a policeman. She was terribly frightened!

She had a brief tenure (one week only) with the Birdseye Family (frozen food fame) on fashionable Eastern Point, Gloucester. Trying to make a fine impression, Ma put forth enormous effort. When it came time to be compensated, the lady of the house said she would be paid two dollars less than the agreed upon amount "because the first week you're only learning." Mother declared that she wouldn't be back. Trying to convince her to stay, Mrs. Birdseye insisted on having her daughter Ruth drive her to the bus line. Mother would never go back!

The Depression era years were certainly difficult for most everyone. Ma told of receiving a shiny dime and an orange for many a Christmas. People in those days were content to have little in the way of material possessions. They were rich in so many other ways.

Mother also worked at Woolworth's, the five-and-dime on Main Street in Gloucester. (Helena Woolworth McCann, the heiress, had made an extra special store according to a Cape Ann historian. Mrs. McCann later purchased the Beauport Mansion on Eastern Point, the eclectic creation of nationally known interior designer, Henry Davis Sleeper.) At first, Ma was behind the nuts and bolts counter of Woolworth's. According to her, there was little to like about that department. She requested a transfer and was changed to the candy counter, which was much more appealing. An oft-recited anecdote by Mother was that, at about the time of her employment, she met her husband-to-be, Matt. A current melody of the time was "I Met a Million Dollar Baby in the Five-and-Ten-Cent Store."

Both a marvelous cook and bowler extraordinaire, over the years, Ma was active in Pigeon Cove Chapel Sewing Circle activities (later the group disengaged from the church and was autonymous), a friends' Card Club, which existed for over fifty years, Women's Club, Pythian Sisters Past Chiefs Club, Finnish Dance Group, Board of Trade, Supper Club with her contemporaries. Rakel Maria Jacobson was born March 18 or 19, 1913 (a family Bible listed the date as March 18, although we always celebrated on March 19).

Ma graduated from Lane Grammar School—Grade Eight—in Gloucester on June 16, 1927. The certificate, signed by Henry Parsons, Mayor—Ernest Fellows, Superintendent, stated that she "has completed the course of study prescribed for the grammar schools and by diligence and correct deportment is entitled to this diploma."

As did many others, Ma had fanciful penmanship. She received a Palmer Method Business Writing certificate—advanced course—for superior ability in rapid muscular movement commercial penmanship — November 17, 1928. She had to leave school after freshman year to help support the family. Most of her earnings supplemented the family pot.

Our family has a confirmation certificate for Mother dated July 7, 1929, and signed by the Lutheran minister, Pastor Ronka. Biblical lessons of course were all in Finnish.

Our precious matriarch, who courageously battled Parkinson's Disease and heart problems, passed away on January 9, 1998, a huge loss for us all remaining. Mother was Dad's valuable counterpart and devotedly indispensable complement. We all loved her so!

Born on September 22, 1913, in the Pigeon Cove Section of Rockport, the patriarch of our family was Matthew (Matti) Hjalmar Kielinen. Because the Yankees here found such ethnic surnames to be tongue twisters, one of my grandfather's quarry bosses actually designated the name of "Mattson" to the family for a spell.

Simple games and athletic activities, such as track and field events at Evans Field, occupied him as a child. Dad told of an acquaintance and a friend once overturning an outhouse with someone doing his business in it on Halloween. That eerie night was for many an evening of tricks.

Dad's work life began when he was about fifteen years of age. His father had died at a young age, succumbing to cancer, and Dad and his brother and sister had to work to help support the family and their mother, Sanna. Earlier in life, Dad had dreamed of becoming an architect. He eventually became an activist in town affairs. Responsible for the 1957 report of the assessors, he found several discrepancies in land and building values and assessments. Dad determined that one assessor had land that he wasn't paying taxes on. Dad was in the plumbing trade—a master plumber—for about twenty-two years and then had a vision of creating Boulder Top—a mélange of summer cottages and small motel overlooking Sandy Bay. It was a Herculean task to take the wild land with scrub pines and huge boulders and convert it into a summer "resort."

Dad was a volunteer fireman, captain at one time, a member of the Granite Pier Committee, Rockport High School Building Committee. (Dad and Russell Brundage were minority members constantly being outvoted by the majority.) Other activities included the Knights of Pythias, State Guard, Chairman of the Town Revaluation Committee (had real estate taxes and abatements printed in book form in 1957), Supper Club, Board of Trade, and Finnish Dance Group. In a way, he achieved his dream of becoming an architect, envisioning and building an enchanting two-story stone house on Granite Street in Pigeon Cove. His mother had given him the plot of land; the granite came from the premises. I was brought home from the hospital to Mother's favorite house at number 243. Starting in 1951, Dad and Mother created Boulder Top from woodland property near the Keystone Bridge.

Dad once told me of his walking on Main Street in Rockport at the time of the sensational murder of Arthur Oker, a tailor, in 1932. Father was about twenty years of age at the time. The killing took place in the middle of the day inside the tailor's shop. The following year, a Stockholm Avenue lady, named Mrs. Augusta Johnson, was brutally murdered in her home on Halloween night. She apparently had gotten a little tipsy, so the story goes, at a church event and said she knew who had killed Mr. Oker the previous year and was ready to reveal it. Later going up the stairs in her home at the corner of Oakland and Stockholm, Mrs. Johnson's killer bludgeoned her with most likely a quarry implement, placed her on her bed, which was set afire. Her gruesome death is still an unsolved mystery in Rockport; to this day many old timers certainly have their speculations but fear being vocal about it.

Our father, Matt Kielinen, died suddenly of a heart attack in October 1963 at the age of fifty, a catastrophic loss to Mother, my sisters, and me. We deeply loved him. His passing was noted on the front page of the *Gloucester Daily Times*, referring to him as the Squire of the North Village and as a leading citizen.

Our parents participated with the Finnish Dance Group members, who had vivid indigenous costumes imported from Finland and were taught the Finn Hop, Raatikko, Polka, Schottische, etc. by Betty Graham and Mrs. Niemi, Miriam Lane's mother. Miriam accompanied with the accordion; Aino Clarke with the violin. The zenith of the dance group's performing days was traveling by bus to Washington, D.C., and dancing at Constitution Hall. The troupe had such a collective spirit of zeal and energy.

The Finnish Dancers reveled in playing pranks on one another. Many years ago, member Bob Graham received a telephone call from the Rockport Post Office informing him that his baby chickens had all arrived and should be picked up. Baffled, the Grahams couldn't understand why they would be receiving a batch of young chicks. The Grahams, not to be outdone, at a later time decided to reciprocate in kind. After a dance rehearsal evening, at a coffee social time at their Rockport residence, Bob and Betty convinced their daughters, demurely clad in pinafores, to pass around savory morsels of varying types. Their guests all oohed and aahed over them. Later in the night, the Grahams asked the visitors, "Did you enjoy the chocolate covered ants?"

Born in 1882 in Finland, Grandfather John Kielinen worked in iron mines out of state, at the Babson Farm Quarry in northern Pigeon Cove, and at the Cape Ann Tool Company in the center of Pigeon Cove Village. He died of cancer at a young age, in his forties. Grandfather, whom we never knew, of course, was sent home to die from the hospital and was in much pain. Pain management was not a thing in those days. According to a newspaper article in 1927, Grandfather Kielinen's funeral was sizeable, with forty automobiles in attendance. Incredible, given the year.

My aunt, Laila Elizabeth Kielinen, born in 1909 in Finland, was Dad's maiden and only sister. She was a domestic at the Phillips Estate at what was then addressed as Mt. Pleasant Avenue according to my recollection. The impressive showplace, owned by Nathan Phillips of LePage's Glue, was located on a promontory overlooking part of Gloucester Harbor. The spacious home, with a grand piano, had the telephone number 25, which a caller gave verbally to an operator. There was a three-car garage for Mrs. Phillips, who had at one time a four-door black expensive sedan. Aunt Laila, or Laila tati in Finnish, traveled to Finland, the country of her birth, in 1951, to take her annual vacation in the winter. Vacation time was dictated by the Phillipses. She became ill in the country of her origin, and her health was thereafter compromised. Aunt Laila passed away prematurely during her forties in 1957.

Laila tati had arrived in Pigeon Cove as a young girl, about twelve years of age. She had been nurtured by her grandmother in Finland and left her only known relatives behind. She got as far as the United States Customs and had to return to Scandinavia. Apparently, the officials at Ellis Island in New York thought she had some kind of disease because of an undetermined skin condition. She came back the next year to stay, according to family lore. She knit all manner of sweaters, mittens, hats, etc. for my sisters, cousins, and me. I know I didn't appreciate all the handiwork that she did!

Born in 1881, Grandmother Sanna (Koivisto) Kielinen—Mummu in Finnish—was my paternal grandmother. I vaguely can picture her. She was a large woman with a white-haired updo and spoke principally her first language, Finnish. According to Dad, she made luscious blackberry shortcakes without the benefit of a recipe. Sunday afternoons, Aunt Sylvia and Uncle John, my parents, and I, and perhaps Aunt Laila, gathered at Mummu's home for coffee with *nisu* (Finnish coffeebread), cake, or pie. I had a special red, white, and blue cup and place at the table and, being the first-born of my generation, was much doted upon by my parents, relatives, and friends. Grandmother attended English for American Citizenship, intermediate class, and was involved in some church activities. Mummu succumbed to stomach cancer in her sixties in 1945.

Born in 1880, Grandmother Mary (Ranta) Jacobson, maternal side, did some household work one summer for iconic actress Helen Hayes in Annisquam. Ma remembered that the grand dame of the stage gave Grandmother a bathrobe as an appreciation gift. Mummu never learned to speak English really, although she attended English class. She did understand quite a bit though. Lanesville was a compact little village with everything anyone could want at one's disposal, plus all her friends were ladies who had emigrated from Finland. Grandmother really did not have to be fluent in English. She wasn't too pleased when her offspring started conversing in America's primary language and she didn't fully comprehend. Her sons Toivo and Walter were born in the old country but came to join the Jacobson family here as young teens.

I can remember staying overnight only once at Mummu Jacobson's house. She often called me "*hyva beka*," meaning good maiden. There was a chamber pot placed under the bed for my two cousins and me sharing the same double bed upstairs. We tee-heed about that! Informing Ma that she had brought up her eight children and Ma could bring up hers, Mummu only babysat for us once. Mummu made time for her women friends. She must have required that camaraderie to maintain her sanity and a sense of balance with her large family. In season, the mothers swam au naturel at Erkkila's Pit in Lanesville.

Mummu told her eldest daughter Sylvia that she couldn't get married to John Kielinen at a certain time and date because Mummu's cow was expecting a calf!

Going back into family genealogy collated by Uncle John Kielinen, it was later discovered that Mummu's mother (nee Nygard; married surname Ranta) had some Swedish blood in her veins. At that time in history, there were "feelings" between the Finns and Swedes! We were never brought up with that heritage. Ma said we were only Finnish and didn't have to mention the Swedish part to anyone.

Born in 1883 in Finland, Grandfather Jacob Jacobson worked in the granite quarries as a paving cutter and quarryman and also at Gloucester Coal. Fari (Grandfather) also operated a pool hall as an avocation in Lanesville on Langsford Street. Ma recalled going to Erkkila's sauna in the woods off High Street—all the family loaded into the Gloucester Coal truck. That must have been quite a sight! According to family photos I've seen, he was a large man. He died young, as he did not want to go to the doctor on a Sunday or holiday because of the extra cost. Grandfather had a ruptured appendix, which consequently cost him his life at a young age in 1933. Relatively soon, a neighbor came to Mummu Jacobson and proposed marriage. Of course, she didn't accept.

Aunt Sylvia (Jacobson) Kielinen was born in 1912 in the United States. Her brother Fred had been awarded the prestigious Sawyer Medal for academic excellence in school. She, too, was deserving of it (had even skipped a grade) but was not bestowed the honor by the powers-that-be because that would mean two people in the same family receiving the award. Times have changed!

Two brothers had married two sisters. My mother Rachel and her sister Sylvia married Matt Kielinen and John Kielinen, respectively. Sylvia was the eldest of the Jacobson girls and often acted as a surrogate mother to her younger siblings. She felt that part of her childhood was robbed from her; rightly so. Very involved in church activities, she was always well versed in current events of the day and an interesting conversationalist. Sylvia tati was a fantastic cook at a time when culinary skills were highly valued. Sadly, she passed away in 1998.

Born in 1912 in Pigeon Cove, Uncle John Kielinen worked at the Cape Ann Tool Company in Pigeon Cove for about forty-five years and served on several town boards including the Board of Health and Cemetery Commission. As a young man, he also was part of the Finnish Athletic Club at Squam Hill Hall, taking part in marching drills, human pyramids, and basketball with local fellows such as brothers Snap and Jim Silva, Bruno Pearson, and Dyke Brown, as well as being involved in track and field events. He divulged to his daughter that one time he swam around the entire periphery of the large Babson Farm Quarry at Halibut Point State Park four times without stopping. Physical fitness was a worthy, sought-after pursuit in those days. During the Bicentennial year, he served on the Scandinavian Committee which scheduled innumerable celebratory events for the community. Planning took over a year. Uncle John left us in 2002 creating a huge void. He was the last of my father's Kielinen family. Luckily, in his retirement, he put together an extensive and valued genealogy of the Kielinen family. He almost reached ninety years of age!

Mother's brothers were Theodore "Cleo," Fred, Toivo, Walter, and Raymond. Uncle Cleo was a fine carpenter with dark hair, Fred a humorous gardener and caretaker of several Annisquam estates, Walter and Toivo worked in the cemetery stone business, and Raymond was a shipper. Raymond ended up passing away on the same day in 1961 as his mother, my grandmother. The unusual occurrence was written up and appeared on page one in the *Gloucester Daily Times*.

Ma's younger sister was Anne, or Enne, in Finnish. Anna Jacobson was involved in an impressive review, instructed by Bernard Pratt at Wainola Hall in Lanesville, according to an April 1934 edition of the local newspaper. Anna, a high school student, performed in "The Parade of the Wooden Soldiers" and the "Virginia Reel." Taking the commercial course, she graduated from Gloucester High School in 1935. A yearbook quote under her picture states, "Shyness is always becoming." Aunt Anna eventually married and became a manager of a high school cafeteria out of town.

Born in 1944, my sister Shirley May O'Maley graduated from Endicott College in Beverly with a degree in Merchandising. She worked for Jordan Marsh in Boston and later received a degree in Interior Design. Shirley and her husband, Bob, successfully brought up their two outstanding sons, Matthew and Mark. Recently, she completed several years of volunteer delivery of Meals on Wheels to the elderly in her town. She spent decades volunteering with an organization which helped the mentally ill, also with church and Scouting committees, as well.

My sister Jane Lila Knight, born in 1947, was awarded collegiate degrees from Salem State University (B.S. in Education) and Northeastern University (Masters in Education) in Boston. Teaching fifth grade briefly, Jane then worked at our family business, Boulder Top, and later helped to manage her husband's engine rebuilding business. At the time of this book writing, for the last seventeen years, she has been the children's librarian in town. Jane and her husband, Rick, are parents of a top-notch son and daughter, Jason and Amy.

I received a Bachelor of Science degree from Salem State College, now University, with a concentration in Liberal Arts and Education, also a general secretarial certificate from Salem Commercial School. Following an eclectic career path, I have worked as an elementary classroom instructor, teacher of English as a Second Language for adults in an evening program, a legal secretary and paralegal, homemaker for elderly clients at a state agency, and a guide at a local house museum which has been designated as a national historic landmark. The love of my life, John Erkkila, and I have been happily married for forty years! As an aside, my real name is Betty (Betty Anne), not Elizabeth. Mother did not want any diminutives of Elizabeth used.

As a postscript, Dad and Ma were part of an anniversary get-together group for several years. The first annual meeting was in 1936 and consisted mostly of relatives, and gatherings continued until the late 1940s. The members had gotten married at about the same time. Generally, they met in the summer, but the initial gathering was on November 1, 1936. The scribe of the group wrote: "weather cool—six couples—fallish with light shower at noon. Home of Sulo and Alice (Erkkila), High Street, Lanesville. Sulo & Alice, Lil & Tibby (Erkkinen), Fred & Fanny (Jacobson), Lil & Pete (Rogers), Walt & Ginny (Martin), Rachel & Matt (Kielinen). Halloween decorations—orange & black theme. Dinner was served in the bedroom, which was emptied of beds, and tables were set up. They had only two rooms at this time. Plans had been made to eat outside but changed because of a shower. The menu consisted of fish chowder, hobgoblin salad, donuts, cider. Football and baseball were played by all in the field beyond. Coffee and a beautiful cake properly inscribed was served in the afternoon. Pictures taken (Betty's note: sometimes posing on the ground in a circle—a la June Taylor dancers—or men in a pyramid). In the evening, home movies were shown by Walker Hancock (Betty's note: neighbor who was a famous sculptor and friend to the Finnish community; also married to a Finnish-American woman, Saima Natti Hancock) at his studio." Other years there was, according to the scribe's notes, "a beach party weenie roast a Long Beach." Sports were played, sometimes with a few selections plinked on the piano. The sweet, simple innocence of it all brings tears to my eyes even now! These couples had little materially but were very blessed in other important ways. They all led useful and exuberant lives.

Years ago, Dad told me about going to the Rendezvous in the 1930s. The outdoor dance platform-type pavilion at Folly Cove was situated on Ipswich Bay, where the sunsets were and are phenomenal. Archival records indicated that two locals, Story Parsons and Laddie Reddy, often ran the dances. Dancers purchased checks and gave a check back for each dance. According to an oral history of Mr. Parsons, "The bands that made money for us were the bands that could knock off twenty dance songs an hour." Adjacent to the dance place was a refreshment stand. A Pigeon Cove civic association, formed in 1935, complained of the noise from "the cheap dance hall" and the musical sounds wafting over the landscape. Some elderly folk today still nostalgically recollect dancing under the stars at the Rendezvous . . . way back when!

We have no photo of Ma in her wedding gown. Perhaps she never posed for a photographic portrait. According to what Mother recorded in a book, "My wedding gown was white chiffon with rhinestone trimmings. I had a silver band on my head for an ornament—April 25, 1936, 7:00 p.m. at home of Rev. Andrew Kuusisto. Then reception at Waino Hall in Lanesville."

They lived as a married couple first at 239R Granite Street, Pigeon Cove in "four cute cozy rooms"—then moved to the stone house Dad and others built at 243 Granite Street on March 30, 1938, then relocating to 110 Phillips Avenue, on October 26, 1944. Later my family changed our residence to Boulder Top, Rockport, a modernistic home Dad built with an incredible view of Sandy Bay below.

Our parents, Matt and Rachel Kielinen, were extremely proud of their Finnish heritage and passed that quality of pride along to their progeny.

Epilogue

The Pigeon Cove section of Rockport is still a pretty-as-a-postcard, serene haven, with few twenty-first century intrusions cropping up. The majority of businesses from fifty or more years ago have vanished, save the remnants of the deserted tool company on Granite Street. The startling luminescent natural beauty remains. Trundling along the rambling Atlantic Shore Path in any season evokes a sensational rush.

Spring is sprinkled in with blaring yellow forsythia and daffodils. Sharing blueberry muffins, coffee, and camaraderie at scenic Andrews Point with old school chums or witnessing the dramatic, show-stopping sunsets at Folly Cove are delights of every summer. Autumn in its dazzling red-and-gilded dress never fails to kindle our senses. The specter of winter's sequined snow glinting on barren oaks and hemlocks is remniscent of a silvery dreamscape. The ocean, at times azure-tinted, scintillant blue or gray, with cumulus or cirrus clouds overhead, creates an irresistible visual impression.

The years from 1941 to 1959 were a quick trip! Subsequent years up to the present time have marched on faster still. Zigzagging through the little roads and lanes of Pigeon Cove, I can still easily recall most of the friendly inhabitants of the houses from decades long past with much affection. Even after the distance of more than half a century, the sweetness of the forever precious memories still lingers. The village and its people helped to shape and define young people of my era, the generation of the 1940s and 1950s. For that cherished gift, I am positively beholden and wholeheartedly grateful!

Readers, may my memoir pique a greater interest in nostalgic and joyful souvenirs from bygone days of your own springtime!

"Though nothing can bring back the hour of splendour in the grass, of glory in the flower, we will grieve not, rather find strength in what remains behind."

William Wordsworth

Historical Timeline

1941 – The saying "Kilroy is here" is popular as is the Lindy Hop, the Conga, and the Kangaroo Jump; actress Hedy Lamar was considered the most beautiful woman in the world; "Button Nose" was Helen O'Connell's nickname – country's best female vocalist; Maxwell House coffee – 33 cents; Four Freedoms – freedom of speech and religion, freedom from want and fear, termed essential by President Roosevelt in speech to Congress January 6; Bing Crosby & Bob Hope star in *The Road to Zanzibar*; German Jews are forced to wear Star of David for easy identification; Joe DiMaggio is sports hero of the year; FDR inaugurated for third term as U.S. President.

1942 – Federal government began forcibly moving 110,000 Japanese-Americans from West Coast to detention camps; Battle of Midway in June was Japan's first major defeat. Movie *Casablanca* starring Humphrey Bogart & Ingrid Bergman released.

1943 – German Field Marshall Rommel & American General Patton face off in North Africa; jitterbugging is a hot dance move & zoot suits have begun to make their appearances in many parts of the country; glamorous Rita Hayworth makes big news when she elopes to marry Orson Welles; popular songs – "As Time Goes By," "Oklahoma," "People Will Say We're in Love"; radio's most popular variety shows – Kate Smith Hour, Stage Door Canteen.

1944 – U.S. and Allied forces invaded Europe at Normandy, France, on D Day, June 6, in greatest amphibious landing in history; GI Bill of Rights providing benefits to veterans was signed by President Roosevelt; representatives of U.S. and major powers met at Dumbarton Oaks, Washington, D.C., to work out formation of postwar world organization that became the United Nations; Franklin Roosevelt elected to fourth term as president.

1945 – President Roosevelt meets with Russia's Stalin & Great Britain's Churchill at Yalta to make postwar plans; Roosevelt dies of cerebral hemorrhage and Harry S. Truman becomes president; after Russian troops surround Berlin, Hitler commits suicide in his bunker; atomic bombs are dropped on Hiroshima and Nagasaki; shoe rationing, meat and butter rationing, and tire rationing end; young Texan Audie Murphy returns home the most decorated soldier of war; songs – "Laura," "June Is Bustin' Out All Over," "Cruising Down the River," "On the Atchison, Topeka & the Santa Fe"; America's most popular movie star – Irish-born actress Greer Garson; top box office – Van Johnson, Roy Rogers, Margaret O'Brien; top radio serials – Helen Trent, Stella Davis, Ma Perkins; Supreme Court outlaws segregation on interstate trains, buses; major trials at Nuremberg, twelve top Nazis to hang, Goering takes poison.

1946 – Churchill's "Iron Curtain" at speech in Missouri; GI Bill helps millions of World War II vets; Bing Crosby, Frank Sinatra, and Perry Como are popular crooners; Philippines given independence by the United States July 4.

1947 – Jackie Robinson first modern black major leaguer and named Rookie of the Year; Howard Hughes unveils his gigantic *Spruce Goose* – largest wingspan of any plane ever built and has room for 700 passengers – only went one mile on one flight; new product – monosodium glutamate, a powder that enhances meat flavor; Polaroid camera that can develop own pictures in sixty seconds makes appearance; *Howdy Doody Show* makes its debut on NBC; hit songs – "Here Comes Santa Claus," "Near You," "Too Fat Polka," "Zip-a-dee-doo-dah"; George Marshall, secretary of state, proposes seventeen billion dollars to rebuild Europe; Ike to head Columbia University; Al Capone dies; Air Force Capt. Chuck Yeager broke sound barrier in X-1 rocket plane.

1948 – Gandhi assassinated for seeking India peace; Russians blockade Berlin; airlift saves city; former band singer Doris Day was signed for her first starring movie role in *Romance on the High Seas*; Truman beats Dewey in historic upset; Milton Berle tops on TV; Kinsey Report on sexuality in the human male published; in art, "Christina's World."

1949 – Clara Bow, the "it girl" of silent movie fame, comes out of retirement briefly to do a local play; developer William Levitt converts potato field in Long Island into suburban community – houses sell for $7,990; Air Force investigates sightings of "flying saucers"; New York Yankees, led by Casey Stangel, win baseball's World Series in five games; the Lone Ranger debuts, as do the Goldbergs, Quiz Kids; North Atlantic Treaty Organization (NATO) established; 45 rpm records are new; hit songs – "Baby It's Cold Outside," "Dear Hearts & Gentle People," "Diamonds Are a Girl's Best Friend," "Rudolf the Red-Nosed Reindeer," "Mule Train," "Some Enchanted Evening"; gasoline is twenty cents a gallon; China, led by Mao, becomes Communist; George Orwell's *1984*; Arthur Miller's *Death of a Salesman* opened on Broadway.

1950 – Mambo and square dancing are popular; *Washington Post* gives President Truman's daughter Margaret a poor review of her vocal concert - the president is incensed enough to write to the critic; products and items first appearing – Miss Clairol, Minute Rice, Diners Club cards; Walt Disney's animated fairytale *Cinderella* enthralls young movie goers; hit singles – "Goodnight, Irene" (the Weavers) and "Be My Love" (Mario Lanza); pacemaker used to revive animal hearts; Boston Brinks, Inc. robbed of $2.8 million; North Korean forces invaded South Korea; variety show *Your Show of Shows* debuted on TV.

1951 – Twenty-second amendment limits presidents to two terms; Truman recalls General Douglas MacArthur, commander of UN forces in Korea, after disagreeing with Truman's Korean War policy; Churchill was prime minister in England; Johnnie Ray's chart topper "Cry" comes in his debut; woman's cotton dress $2.98; *I Love Lucy* TV debut; book J.D. Salinger's *Catcher in the Rye*; Jordan's King Abdullah assassinated.

1952 – new in this year – felt tip markers, Holiday Inns, Cinerama; Dr. Jonas Salk begins testing a vaccine against polio; Eva "Evita" Peron, beloved First Lady of Argentina, dies; Willie Sutton – a "very polite" bank robber is captured; movies – *Singing in the Rain, High Noon, the Snows of Kilimanjaro*; George VI dies; Elizabeth II queen of England; Fulgencio Batista overthrows Cuban government; Charlie Chaplin denied re-entry to U.S.; Richard Nixon, as vice-president, gave Checkers speech, so called because of sentimental reference to his dog Checkers; NBC's "Today" show premiered, with Dave Garroway as host.

1953 – Korean War ends; Scrabble becomes a fad; General Motors introduces the Corvette; John F. Kennedy, age thirty-six, announces engagement to twenty-three-year-old Jacqueline Bouvier; Sophie Tucker, the "Last of the Red Hot Mamas," celebrates her fifty years in show business; 3-D movie fad is big this year with films like *House of Wax*; new words and phrases – name dropper, cookout, split-level, egghead, jet stream; Stalin dies in U.S.S.R.; Hugh Hefner starts *Playboy*; Julius and Ethel Rosenberg, guilty of conspiracy to commit wartime espionage, executed at Sing Sing Prison; California Governor Earl Warren sworn in as fourteenth chief justice of the U.S. Supreme Court.

1954 – 1st atomic sub Nautilus launched; Puerto Rican terrorists shoot five congressmen on House floor; Supreme Court rules school segregation unconstitutional; *Forrestal*, aircraft carrier, is largest warship ever built; Fess Parker stars as Davy Crockett on ABC show; Ronald Reagan to host Sunday night *General Electric Theater*; hit songs – "3 Coins in the Fountain," "Teach Me Tonight," "Shake Rattle & Roll," "Mambo Italiano," "Cara Mia"; *Father Knows Best* debuts on television; *On the Waterfront* wins eight Oscars; TV dinners introduced; book – Tolkien, *Lord of the Rings*.

1955 – Richard Daley elected Chicago mayor; Albert Einstein dies; civil rights: Rosa Parks sparks bus boycott after refusing to give her seat to a white man in Alabama; James Dean dies; AFL-CIO to merge under George Meany; Ike has heart attack; Princeton hires first Negro instructor; Grace Kelly stars in *The Country Girl*; songs – "Rock Around the Clock," "Mr. Sandman," "16 Tons," "Yellow Rose of Texas."

1956 – Italian liner *Andrea Doria* sinks, is rammed by Swedish-American liner *Stockholm* off Nantucket; Rocky Marciano retires as champion; Nikita Khruschev, first secretary of Communist Party, denounces Stalin; Soviet forces crush anti-Communist revolt in Hungary; Elvis Presley makes appearance from waist up on *Ed Sullivan Show*; coffee – sixty-nine cents a pound; *Marty* wins Academy Award for best picture; big movie is Mike Todd's production of Jules Verne tale, *Around the World in 80 Days*; on Broadway, *My Fair Lady* with Julie Andrews.

1957 – Governor Faubus sends National Guard to keep nine Negroes from Little Rock Central High School; U.S.S.R. puts *Sputnik* satellite in orbit; Ford Thunderbird one of hot cars; JFK awarded Pulitzer Prize for his book *Profiles in Courage*; premiered TV show *American Bandstand* hosted by Dick Clark; hits songs – "A White Sports Coat" (& a Pink Carnation), "April Love," "Bye Bye Love," "Diana," "Love Letters in the Sand," "That'll Be the Day," "You Send Me," "Wake Up Little Susie"; Althea Gibson first black woman to win tennis championship at Wimbledon; new TV show – *Perry Mason*; new this year – retractable convertible (Ford Sunliner), Edsel auto; Asian flu; cancer tied to smoking according to U.S. Surgeon General.

1958 – Alaska voted into statehood, actual January 3, 1959; Nelson Rockefeller new New York governor; hula hoops craze sweeps country; Nash Rambler car sells well; Pan American offers first regularly scheduled jet service to Europe; American Express introduces the credit card; VP Richard Nixon's tour of South American countries meets with violent reception in Peru and Venezuela; Russian author Boris Pasternak sells 450,000 copies of his book *Dr. Zhivago* in U.S.; World's Fair held in Brussels, Belgium; TV's *77 Sunset Strip* with Edd "Kookie" Byrnes; popular songs – "All I Have to Do Is Dream," "Bird Dog," "Pink Shoe Laces," "Chanson d'Amour," "Volare"; Joanne Woodward, twenty-seven, and Paul Newman, thirty-three, married; presidential aide Sherman Adams resigned over scandal involving alleged improper gifts; first domestic jet airline passenger service in U.S. opened by National Airlines between New York and Miami.

1959 – Mass murderer Charles Starkweather executed; Hawaii becomes fifieth state; Fidel Castro assumed power January 1; fads – black leotards and parachute jumping, youngsters wearing western outfits; Thanksgiving time rumors of contaminated cranberries – changed holiday menu of millions; rock & roll world stunned by deaths of Buddy Holly, Ritchie Valens, and the Big Bopper in plane crash; *Gidget* – popular acclaim starring Sandra Dee as a California teenager; St. Lawrence Seaway opens; William Wyler's *Ben-Hur* released; "payola" scandals – number of radio disk jockeys admit taking cash payments in exchange for playing certain songs.

Nicknames

Below is a smattering of the nicknames used by various members of the high school classes from 1954 to 1959. Many of the appellations still exist to this very day.

Joydee	Joyce Anderson
Rut	Russell Allen
Beetle	James Blake
Red	Carol Garrett
Pete	Francis Leahy
Peanut	Susan Reilly
Janska	Janette Schreiber
Bobbie	Ann Seavey
Ray Ray	Raymond Smith
Klineberg	Ado Torrisi
Butch	Homer Sweet
Fifi	Phyllis Lane
Bunny	Marilyn MacLeod
Weezie	Louise Perkins
Pear	Ralph Parady
Hot Toddy	Charles Anderson
Tee-Dee	Cynthia Hillier
Annabelle	Ann Broadley
Mev	Mary Evelyn Brown
Herrin' Choker	Thomas Cavanaugh
Lover-Boy	Charlie Elwell
Bubbles	Jean Erickson
Spindle	Roy Spurlin

Zorro	Albert Lattof
Little Iodine	Loretta Conigliari
Smiley	Marie Cunningham
Russian	June Fears
Honka	John Grimes
Rip	Norman Hannibal
Linda-Finn	Linda Komi
Reverend	Henry Koski
Frenchy	Pat Theriault
Tink	Mary Jane Francis
Willie	Frances Wilson
Bette	Betty Kielinen

THE FINNISH LANGUAGE

Most people in Finland (about ninety-three percent) speak Finnish, a language related to Estonian and distantly to Hungarian. The language is entirely phonetic. Umlauts are sometimes used. Finnish utilizes a great number of compound words. In all words, the stress falls on the first syllable.

Below are some English words with their Finnish equivalents:

Monday – *maanantai*; Thursday – *torstai*; Saturday – *lauantai*; June – *kesäkuu*; July – *heinäkuu*; December – *joulukuu* (days of week and months usually are not capitalized)

house – *talo*; street – *katu*; boy – *poika*; beautiful – *kaunis*; girl – *tyttö*; thank you – *kiitos*; Mr. – *herra*; Ms. – *neiti*; telephone – *puhelin*; Finland – *Suomi*;

one – *yksi*; five – *viisi*; hundred – *sata*; zero – *nolla*; thousand – *tuhat*; half – *puoli*; dictionary – *sanakirja* (which translates to word book)

I want to learn to speak Finnish better. (*Haluan oppia puhumaan suomea paremmin.*)

Drive slowly! (*Aja hitaasti!*)

Where can we go dancing? (*Mihin voimme mennä tanssimaan?*)

What time is it? (*Kuinka paljon kello on?*)

In July, James Brown intends to drive by car to the most important tourist spots in Finland. (*Heinäkuussa James Brown aikoo tehdä automatkan Suomen tarkeimpiin matkailukohteisiin.*)

Like other languages, Finnish has borrowed from English:

filmi; kamera; pankki; sampoo; tomaatti; stressi; trendi; festivaalit; firma; fax; gramma

Both Finnish and Swedish are the official languages of Finland. The tongues differ vastly from one another. All official communications from the state administration and national institutions appear in both languages. Road signs are usually in Finnish and Swedish. All Finns learn English in school and generally have a good knowledge of it. The Finnish people respect silence and are comfortable with it.

About the Author

My Little Chickadee is an enchanting memoir encompassing the time slice of 1941 to 1959. Coming of age as a shy, unassuming girl of Finnish-American descent, Betty Kielinen Erkkila conjures up reminiscences about home, school, and church life in Rockport, Massachusetts. One chapter harkens back to her parents' lives during the 1920s and 1930s in Lanesville and Pigeon Cove.

Pursuing an eclectic career path, Betty has been engaged as an elementary school instructor, legal secretary, English as a Second Language teacher for adults, homemaker/shopper for elderly clients, and a guide at a historic house museum. She fancies (delights in) Finnish language study, travel, music, and reading. Betty and her husband, John, reside in the Pigeon Cove section of Rockport.

Perhaps the author's memories will inspire you to jot down your own recollections as a family gift and legacy.